Mom Set Free

GOOD NEWS FOR MOMS
WHO ARE TIRED OF TRYING
TO BE GOOD ENOUGH

BIBLE STUDY

JEANNIE CUNNION

LifeWay Press® Nashville, Tennessee

Published by LifeWay Press® • ©2017 Jeannie Cunnion • Reprinted July 2018

ISBN 978-1-4300-3961-7

Item 005720367

Dewey decimal classification: 649

Subject heading: MOTHERHOOD \ PARENTING \ STRESS (PSYCHOLOGY)

To order additional copies of this resource, write LifeWay Church Resources Customer Service; One LifeWay Plaza; Nashville, TN 37234-0113; FAX order to 615.251.5933; call toll-free 800.458.2772; email orderentry@lifeway.com; order online at www.lifeway.com; or visit the LifeWay Christian Store serving you.

Printed in the United States of America

Adult Ministry Publishing, LifeWay Church Resources, One LifeWay Plaza, Nashville, TN 37234-0152

CONTENTS

ABOUT THE AUTHOR

Jeannie Cunnion is the author of *Parenting the Wholehearted Child* and *Mom Set Free* and a frequent speaker at women's conferences and parenting events around the country. Her passion is encouraging women to live in the freedom for which Christ has set us free—a message her own heart needs to be reminded of daily.

Jeannie holds a Master's degree in Social Work, and her writing has been featured on outlets such as *The Today Show, Fox News, The 700 Club,* and *Focus on the Family.*

As a self-described grace-clinger, Jeannie's writing is woven with humility, honesty, humor, and a contagious love for the good news.

Jeannie lives in Connecticut with her husband, Mike, and their four boys.

Connect with Jeannie at:

Facebook/Instagram/Twitter: JeannieCunnion

Blog: JeannieCunnion.com

DEAR FELLOW MOM,

I am so grateful that you have chosen to invest your precious time into this study. While I may not have the privilege of knowing you personally, I bet we have a few things in common. I bet we both desperately love our kids. I bet we both desperately want to get this parenting thing right for them. I bet we also both feel like we are under so. much. pressure. Every day we feel it. We are daily bombarded with covert and overt messages that challenge us to achieve the unachievable as moms—to "be enough" for our children.

But here's the thing. We don't just feel the pressure to "be enough" for our kids. We feel the pressure to "be enough" for God, in and through our parenting. Indeed, the pressure runs both horizontal and vertical, leaving us worried that we are not only letting down our kids, but also fearful that we are disappointing God. And ultimately the pressure steals the joy and the wonder from our parenting.

I speak from experience on this one. I was trying to keep God's love through my good behavior, and I also raised my three young boys through that lens. I was striving to achieve a goodness of my own, and I was putting that same pressure on my kids. Grace, real grace, was lost on me. I believe that is where most of us get stuck. In all our striving, we will keep failing. I did.

From the outside, it may have looked like I was pulling it off. But on the inside, I was desperate, overwhelmed, ashamed, and hopeless because I was realizing how incapable I was of being the perfect Christian woman, wife, and mom I'd set out to be.

Oh friend, if you're a mom who is tired of striving to be "good enough," lean in. I have such good news for us. Freedom from the pressure that seeks to weigh us down and wipe us out—the freedom that you and I are desperate for—isn't found in our striving to be better moms tomorrow but in the good news of God's grace today.

The good news of the gospel changes how we live and therefore how we parent. We can't live in one truth and parent from another. If we want to raise children who live from the freedom found in being wholeheartedly loved by God, we have to know the freedom for which Christ has set us free (Gal. 5:1).

Before we get started I want you to know that I am on this journey alongside you. There is still so much for me to learn. That being said, there are a few heart-changing and freedom-full truths God has been teaching me that I am so excited to share with you.

Are you ready to breathe deeper and walk lighter and enjoy your parenting journey more?

Are you ready to parent as a mom set free? Me too. Let's dive in.

Jeannie

We can't live in one truth and parent from another.

#MOMSETFREE

FREEDOM FROM THE PRESSURE TO BE ENOUGH

Each week, you'll find group discussion questions here. Use these to kick-start conversation with your Bible study group.

Group Discussion Questions

1. If you could go back to the time when you were preparing for your first child, what advice would you give to the younger you?

2. What are some of the pressures moms face each day?

3. What weaknesses has parenting revealed to you as a mom? What is the hardest part of being a mom for you?

4. What are your biggest worries and concerns when you think you are not enough for your kids or for God?

5. Read Isaiah 26:3. What do you learn from this verse?

6. What does it mean to rely on the peace and power of God? How would that reliance change your parenting?

7. What do you want to gain most from this Bible study and this group? How can the group pray for you?

_____

_____

_____

_____

To hear more from Jeannie, download the optional video bundle at lifeway.com/momsetfree

When was the last time you remember saying to another mom something like, "You know, this parenting thing isn't that hard after all. I mostly feel like I've got it mastered, and the pressure to get it all right doesn't really phase me. I don't know why everyone else thinks it's so complicated and exhausting"?

We are under so much pressure.

You can't remember saying that? OK, good. Because neither can I. In fact, I've never said that.

What I can remember saying to another mom is that I am so overwhelmed, I mostly feel like I have no idea what I'm doing, and I often feel like I get it wrong. Don't let that concern you, as this isn't a study about how to be like me. If it were, we'd be in big trouble. This is a study about how to parent freely in the assurance of and reliance on the sovereignty and grace of God. And rest assured, I have to go back to the good news every single day in order to live and parent that way. Because I, like you, feel the pressure.

We are under so much pressure.

Our pressure-cooker culture tells us we have to "be enough" for our kids. Or worse, that we actually *can* be enough for our kids, if we just try hard enough. We are told that their hearts are wholly reliant on our performance, and their entire futures are riding on our ability to perfectly orchestrate their lives. In other words, we are told that if we get it all right, our kids will turn out all right. And if we get it all wrong, our kids will turn out all wrong.

Well, if we're going to get honest (and my hope is that we are going to get really, really honest in our seven weeks together), we will admit that we rarely feel like we're enough and we often feel like we're getting it wrong.

Pause here and rank where you land on some of the common pressures we face. Circle where you fall on a scale of 1 to 5, with 1 being "no pressure" and 5 being "immense pressure."

The pressure to <u>orchestrate</u> a picture-perfect future for your children

1   2   3   4   5

The pressure to be a <u>perfect example</u> for your children to follow

1   2   3   4   5

The pressure to <u>create</u> a saving and vibrant faith in your children's lives

1   2   3   4   5

The pressure to <u>produce</u> Christlike character in your children's lives

1   2   3   4   5

The pressure to <u>shield</u> your children from the ungodly influence of culture

1   2   3   4   5

The pressure to <u>protect</u> your children from hardship and/or suffering

1   2   3   4   5

The pressure to <u>ensure</u> your children fulfill their full potential and purpose

1   2   3   4   5

The pressure to <u>prove</u> you have it all together in front of other moms

1   2   3   4   5

The pressure to <u>earn</u> God's pleasure in the way you parent your children

1   2   3   4   5

Are there any other pressures you experience that aren't listed above? Describe them.

Is it just me or was even the mere exercise of thinking about these pressures exhausting and overwhelming? If you'll notice, each one of the pressures we ranked holds an impossible standard or unrealistic expectation, which I underlined. During this week and next, we will dig into each one of these pressures and speak

God's promises over them. But for now, I want us to have a clear picture of just how much pressure we are under, and even more importantly, where this pressure leaves us stuck.

The pressure leaves us stuck bouncing between worry and fear, with clenched fists that are trying to control outcomes. It leaves us stuck feeling guilty about all that we're not, compared to what every other mom *seems* to be. It leaves us stuck feeling angry—angry that no matter how hard we try, we aren't getting the results the parenting books promised us we'd get if we followed the right steps. It leaves us ashamed—ashamed over our shortcomings and weaknesses that are daily revealed through our mothering. And ultimately, it leaves us hopeless. Why? Well, mostly because all of our hope is in us.

We think that if we just keep trying harder to be better examples and do more for our kids, we will finally become the moms we long to be. But, we're exhausted. This is just no way to live and parent. It's not how our heavenly Father created us to live and parent. But there is a better way.

We are going to start to discover the better way by turning to 2 Corinthians. This book of the Bible was a letter written by the apostle Paul to the church in Corinth. The Corinthian church was comprised of mostly inconsistent believers who had embraced a false gospel and were experiencing affliction. Paul wrote to them as someone who was well acquainted with affliction, and out of his great love for these people, he pleaded with them to embrace the true gospel.

So while Paul was not writing directly to moms in the twenty-first century who are under immense pressure, experiencing affliction, and trying to raise children in the truth of the gospel, I think we will see how his writing and encouragement apply to our daily lives.

> *We don't want you to be unaware, brothers and sisters, of our affliction that took place in Asia. We were completely overwhelmed—beyond our strength—so that we even despaired of life itself. Indeed, we felt that we had received the sentence of death, so that we would not trust in ourselves but in God who raises the dead. He has delivered us from such a terrible death, and he will deliver us. We have put our hope in him that he will deliver us again.*
> 2 CORINTHIANS 1:8-10

The apostle Paul understood pressure. Note what he said in verse 8. In the NIV translation, Paul writes, *"We were under great pressure, far beyond our ability to endure, so that we despaired of life itself."*

Maybe it sounds dramatic, but there have been plenty of days when I have felt pushed far beyond my ability to endure in motherhood. No, my life was not at stake like Paul's, and my circumstances were far less severe. But there have been some very hard and dark days when the enemy has flaunted my weaknesses and failures before me, and I have been swallowed up by despair.

> Have you ever felt the pressure you are under in your mothering is far beyond your ability to endure? Describe that here in a few words.

In verse 9, Paul showed us what pressure and peril are intended to do. He wrote in the NIV, *"But this happened that we might not rely on ourselves but on God, who raises the dead."*

Oh friend, how applicable this is to our parenting. The pressure we are under is intended to make us rely on God.

And here's the thing. So much of the pressure we experience and so many of the emotions in which we get stuck, stem from us getting this backward. The pressure stems from believing that parenting is about God relying on us to be enough for our kids. But that's not it at all.

Parenting is about us relying on God to be enough for our children and for us.

> What does relying on God look like for you in your parenting?

God wants our hope set on Him, not on us.

What causes you to rely on yourself rather than on God? What is typically the result of that?

This passage can teach us to rely on God when we feel overwhelmed. Becoming the mom we long to be doesn't happen by trying harder and being better and doing more to be enough for our kids. It happens by relying more on God, who already is enough.

Now notice how Paul concluded this passage. He essentially said, *Hey, don't forget! God has shown up before, so rest assured He will show up again and again. On Him we must set our hope.*

According to the *Evangelical Dictionary of Biblical Theology*, the definition of *hope* is "to trust in, wait for, look for, or desire something or someone; or to expect something beneficial in the future."[1]

What are some things you place your hope in every day?

What has been the result?

Where does Scripture tell us our hope should come from?

If there is anything I've discovered about myself in the last couple of years, it's that my sense of discouragement and sadness means I've put my hope back in my hands. Hopelessness is always my cue to recite **PSALM 42:11**—a verse I had to memorize to get my hope back where it belongs. *"Why am I discouraged? Why is my heart so sad? I will put my hope in God. I will praise him again—my Savior and my God"* **(NLT).**

God wants our hope set on Him, not on us. He wants us to rely on Him and trust Him with the children He has entrusted to us.

Read 1 Thessalonians 5:24. Who is doing the action in these verses?

What is the promise?

We'll talk more about this tomorrow but before we close out our day, I want to remind you of something us moms are good at forgetting. He who called you to motherhood will be faithful to see you through motherhood. God chose you on purpose to parent the children He has gifted to you. I know it may not always seem like it. Whether you're wrangling toddlers who refuse to cooperate, wiping the tears of your teenager caused by situations you can't fix, or disciplining your children for the hundredth time today and wondering if there will ever come a day when they will listen and obey without a fight, you may think God could have chosen someone better for your kids. Trust me, I get it. But those thoughts are from the enemy whose specialty is feeding us lies. He wants to see us suffocate under the pressure of parenting.

What we have to remember is that God did not choose us to be our children's Savior. He chose us to be our children's parents. And He will equip us to parent the children He has entrusted to us.

CLOSE WITH PRAYER

Father, how freeing it is to know that You are not relying on me to be enough for my kids. But instead You want me to rely on You to be enough for both of us. God, help me remember that You are my hope and help me put my hope in You alone. *"Now may the God of hope fill you with all joy and peace as you believe so that you may overflow with hope by the power of the Holy Spirit"* **(ROM. 15:13).**

I stumbled from my bed to the medicine cabinet to find something, anything, that would relieve my son's pain. Through squinted, burning eyes, I read the time on the clock as I entered the bathroom. 2 a.m. Only a mere hour after he'd last woken up in pain, and I'd soothed him to sleep with back scratching and prayers for healing. I don't know when we fell back to sleep again, but I do know the sun came up too quickly and greeted me with a to-do list that I'd be lucky to tackle on a good night's sleep.

I don't want to treat my blessings as burdens.

Before my feet hit the floor I prayed, *I will not treat my blessings as burdens. Lord, help me. I don't want to treat my blessing as burdens.* My heart was centered, but reality still loomed. Our refrigerator was empty. The new puppy needed exercise. I had a meal to cook for my neighbor who was ill, and I had fifty emails to return. But before that, I'd still need to make breakfast and get the other boys out the door with a smile on my face and a prayer on my lips. We wouldn't have time to read our devotion that morning. We'd barely have time to breathe. My insides groaned, "I can't. I must. But I can't."

Maybe you've had a morning like this? The kind where you are painfully aware that the physical and mental demands of parenting are going to push you far beyond your human limitations, and you're once again assured, "I am not enough for this. Definitely not enough."

Share your most recent experience here.

In the early stages of writing this study—actually at a very crucial point when the enemy was hurling lies at my heart about how I'm the only mom who feels *this* inadequate—I came across a photo on Instagram posted by my friend Heather.

It was a photo of Heather's hand holding a note card with **ROMANS 12:2** written on it. The card read, *"Instead, fix your attention on God. You'll be changed from the inside out" (MSG).*

Under the photo Heather confessed that "her soul has carried around the 500-pound lie that it's all up to her to control the outcomes" in her life and her parenting, and how God was leading her to surrender the burden to Him. Heather then invited other women to comment about the lies that were creeping into their minds so she could encourage them with God's truth and pray for them.

I was curious to see what other moms had said, so I scrolled down to the comment section. What I discovered was an undeniable theme among the long list of responses.

Mom after mom confessed to feeling like they're not enough. Here, in fact, is what three of the moms shared:

- Any other mom could do it better.

- I'm not good enough.

- I can't do this mothering thing one more day.

These three responses very much represent the others who wrote about feeling defeated and overwhelmed.

How did you feel reading those responses?

How would you answer Heather's question: "What lies are creeping into your mind as you parent?"

From where do you think those lies stem? Are they self-imposed? From society? From specific people in your life?

Now remember with me The Message paraphrase Heather shared of Romans 12:2.

We are urged to do what?

And what is the benefit of that?

Oh friend, what more could we ask for? In these seven weeks together, we are going to fix our attention on God, push back the pressure with the truth of God's Word, and be transformed from the inside out—transformed into moms set free from the pressure to be good-enough—for our children and for God, and moms who live in the assurance that who God is, and what He gives us, *is enough*.

I'm certainly not suggesting that the pressure to be enough and do enough is going away. The pressure you felt when you started your homework today is the same pressure that will be waiting for you when you finish. (I'm sorry about that.) We simply can't make the pressure go away. But we don't have to let it dictate how we live and how we parent. That's the difference—and it's a radical one.

God has a simple but profound message for us regarding our quest to be enough.

READ PSALM 46:10 (NIV):
*Be still, and know that I am God; I will be exalted among the nations,
I will be exalted in the earth.*

Oh, how profound this is for our lives and for our parenting. God is firmly but tenderly wanting us to hear Him assure us, *Enough, my dear daughter, of trying to be enough. Know that I, not you, am God. And I am good at being God.*

Let's personalize this for our parenting. What are your thoughts and emotions as you ponder this verse?

Obviously this isn't a charge to be permanently and physically still. Can we consider the ramifications of that for a moment and get a giggle out of the picture we're getting in our minds? I once heard a story about a woman who read this verse in her morning devotion and then decided to "be still" that day and not do any of the usual things she does every day to care and provide for her family. She let them prepare their breakfast before school. She didn't clean up or care for the home and she didn't make dinner. And when her husband returned home that evening, he asked, "Honey, what in the world happened today?" and she responded, "I read Psalm 46:10 in which God said 'be still' so I obeyed."

So we're clear that is not the kind of "be still" God is talking about, right?

I have actually clung to this verse for years. In fact, I have this verse written on a sticky note just above my desk because, as a girl prone to striving to be enough, I need to be reminded of this truth every day. On the note I wrote the NASB Bible translation, which says, *"Cease striving and know that I am God."*

Let's not miss this. We can stop striving to be enough, because who God is (sovereign) and what God gives us in the person and work of Jesus Christ (grace) is enough.

Please read that again. This is hugely important to our study. Now fill in the blank below to make sure we've got this.

> Who God is, which is _____, and what God gives us, which is _____, is enough.

God for us, and Christ in us, is all the enough we need.

In anchoring our hope in this good news, we will find relief from the pressure that is creeping in and threatening to steal the joy and the adventure from our parenting.

> Read Matthew 11:28-30.

What I love most about this passage is that it is a personal invitation from Jesus. These are His words, not mine. It doesn't get any better than that.

> What does Jesus invite us to do?

What does Jesus tell us about His heart in these verses?

What does He tell us He will give us?

The word for *yoke* in this passage is used in other parts of the New Testament as a contrast to grace and freedom (Acts 15:10; Gal. 5:1). Some believe Jesus is comparing His yoke to the yoke of the law in this passage, telling His followers to put down the burden of trying to live up to impossible standards and take on a lighter yoke, the yoke of grace.

In Eugene Peterson's The Message, Jesus' invitation is beautifully translated.

Let's read it together, but before we do, please insert your name at the beginning of the verse.

> _____, *Are you tired? Worn out? Burned out on religion? Come to me. Get away with me and you'll recover your life. I'll show you how to take a real rest. Walk with me and work with me—watch how I do it. Learn the unforced rhythms of grace. I won't lay anything heavy or ill-fitting on you. Keep company with me and you'll learn to live freely and lightly.*
> MATTHEW 11:28-30, MSG

The "real rest" Jesus is talking about here isn't simply a good long nap in the middle of the day. (Although, that is always fantastic.) It's not a rest in which you simply clear the kids' calendar and cancel all your plans. (Although, sometimes that is fantastic, too.) The kind of rest Jesus offers is much more profound. This rest is one where our soul is at rest in the midst of motherhood. It's a rest that enables us to live, as Jesus concluded, freely and lightly.

Doesn't just the very idea of living freely and lightly make you take a long, deep breath of relief? Or maybe it makes you skeptical. Maybe you think, *I am under way too much pressure, and falling way too short, to ever live freely and lightly as a mom. There is entirely too much I need to do. There are meals to cook. Bottoms to wipe. College applications to complete. Schedules to coordinate. Carpools to run.*

Hugs to give. Appointments to make. Games to watch. Emails to check. And that's just the easy stuff. Don't even get me started on the hard and complicated stuff.

If that's you, I get it. But friend, Jesus never invites us into anything He can't make good on. He is a promise keeper through and through. And you are not exempt from His promises. He is personally inviting you to live as a mom set free.

> Now please read Matthew 11:28-30 again, and note the ways Jesus says we will learn to live freely and lightly.

Are you noticing a theme among your answers? We learn to live freely and lightly by abiding in Him, not by trying to be Him. It happens by coming to know Him better and better (see Col. 1:10). More on that tomorrow.

CLOSE WITH PRAYER

Father, You are so good and so generous. You have invited us to Yourself, just as we are, not as we wish we were. Tired, worn-out, burned out, having made mistakes, and needing rest. Real rest. Rest only You can provide and rest You give without hesitation or expectation.

DAY 3

We left off yesterday with a truth you're going to hear me say often. It is the one God embedded into my heart to be the foundation of this study: who God is and what He gives us is enough.

So today, we are going to pick back up with this truth and continue to explore the game-changing significance this holds for our parenting. This is big picture stuff, but it's foundational to the rest we crave. Then we'll get down into the nitty-gritty of the specific pressures we face.

When praying for my kids, I have always used the words, "my boys" or "my sons." There is, of course, nothing wrong with praying this way. God entrusted these boys to my husband and me to raise to His glory. But on one particular and unforgettable night, while crying out to God about a painful hardship one of my boys was facing and feeling completely incompetent to help him navigate it, I felt the Holy Spirit remind me that these boys are first and foremost sons of God. That as much as I love them and long for them, they were created by Him, they belong to Him, and His love and desire for them is infinitely more profound and pure than even mine. In light of this truth, I began to pray "Your sons," rather than "my sons" to be reminded that He is their all-knowing, all-powerful Father. And because God is sovereign and full of grace, He can be trusted with the children He has entrusted to me.

I truly believe that it is only when we surrender to this truth that we will finally be free and empowered to thrive in our mothering. We have to know what Scripture says and trust the power it holds to free us (Matt. 22:29).

So I want us to look at a few key passages that speak to the sovereignty and good-ness of God. Though it would be fair to say the whole Bible speaks to this, we will hone in on just a few passages that we can apply to our parenting.

READ EPHESIANS 1:17-19a (NIV):
17 I keep asking that the God of our Lord Jesus Christ, the glorious Father, may give you the Spirit of wisdom and revelation, so that you may know him better. 18 I pray that the eyes of your heart may be enlightened in order that you may know the hope to which he has called you, the riches of his glorious inheritance in his holy people, 19 and his incomparably great power for us who believe.

Paul prayed that God would give "the Spirit of wisdom and revelation, so that" we may _____.

What three things did Paul pray for the Ephesians to know in verses 18-19?

I want you to know this is my prayer for us today. In fact, I'd really love for us to start today by praying God would do this for us as we search Scripture on the sovereignty and grace of God. Will you join me in praying this together?

Father, we beg You to give us the spirit of wisdom and revelation, so that we may come to know You better. Lord, how can we trust You and rely on You if we don't know You? We pray that the eyes of our hearts may be enlightened in order that we may know the hope to which You have called us, the riches of Your grace, and the incomparably great power for us who believe. Amen.

How have you tended to think about God's sovereignty? How has your understanding of God's sovereignty impacted the way you parent?

Look up the following verses, and note what they have to say about God's power.

Psalm 139:16

Proverbs 16:9

Isaiah 55:8

Ephesians 1:11-12

Revelation 1:8

READ MATTHEW 7:9-11:

Who among you, if his son asks him for bread, will give him a stone? Or if he asks for a fish, will give him a snake? If you then, who are evil, know how to give good gifts to your children, how much more will your Father in heaven give good things to those who ask him.

Sometimes we view God as someone who wants to take things away from us. How does this passage refute that lie?

How can we apply this truth to our children?

READ ROMANS 8:32:

He did not even spare his own Son but offered him up for us all. How will he not also with him grant us everything?

What does this verse reveal about God's ability to understand the sadness, grief, and even anguish that we experience as parents?

This is the truth we have to remember when our children are bullied or rejected by their peers, when they are battling sin and temptation, when their feelings get hurt or their hearts get broken, when they struggle with substance abuse or eating disorders, when they make wrong choices, or when they simply don't feel lovable or valuable. When our hearts break for our kids and we long to right every wrong in their lives, we have to remember they have a sovereign and good heavenly Father.

What are some of the battles you are facing alongside your children right now that you desperately wish you could fix or control?

How do these verses encourage you or breathe hope into those situations?

To say that God is sovereign is not to say that our children don't have free will. Indeed, God has given all of us free will. We are all responsible for the choices we make, and our choices matter. However, God is not limited by our choices. He is continually working everything together *"for the good of those who love God and are called according to his purpose for them"* **(ROM. 8:28, NLT).** More on that verse later. But for now, I want us to see something essential to our journey to freedom.

Remembering our good Father's sovereignty relieves so much of the pressure we experience in motherhood. It's not all up to you, and it's not all up to me—and praise Him for that!

I desperately needed to be reminded of this recently on a terrible day at the end of a difficult week. A week that entailed bad grades in school for one of my boys, bad words in the schoolyard for another, and bad dreams at night for another. Throw in bad teething for Baby Finn and you have quite the concoction. I joke, but these things break my mama heart, and they threaten to break my spirit. We give these boys everything we've got, we guide them in truth, we encourage them to use their God-given gifts to the fullest, we try to model godly living, we pray, we pray, and we pray, but ultimately we have to face that we are powerless to control the outcome, so we put our trust in our all-powerful God.

Let's turn to one more passage that demonstrates God's all-sufficient power.

Read 2 Chronicles 20:1-12.

The Moabites, the Ammonites, and some of the Meunites were descending upon Judah to fight. Verse 3 says *"Jehoshaphat was afraid."*

If we're honest, there are days of motherhood that look like this. Instead of all the –ites, our battles look like the things we named earlier, and we are afraid.

How did Jehoshaphat prepare for battle in verse 3?

Now record how Jehoshaphat ended his prayer to the Lord in verse 12.

We do not know what to do, but our eyes are on You.

If there ever was a prayer for us to pray when we feel powerless and afraid, I think we've just found it: *"we have no power ... we do not know what to do, but our eyes are on you"* (NIV).

How would this mind-set impact your daily parenting?

Just imagine how much deeper we'd breathe (and how much better we'd sleep) if we had the prayer of Jehoshaphat on repeat. How often do we not know what to do? Or feel powerless over the things our kids are facing and navigating? And we think it's all up to us to figure it out, solve it, and be their rescuer. We are trying to fill shoes in their lives that only fit their heavenly Father. The invitation to us is to rely on God, fix our eyes on Him, and trust the enoughness of God in our kids' lives.

And yet. What I find so beautiful, so humbling, and perhaps, at times, so frightening, is that God chooses to use us, to involve us, in the work He is doing in the lives of our children. God is not asking us to play His role. Yes, we are significant in their lives—oh so very significant. But we are not sovereign. We can be instruments of grace while we rest in the assurance that God already has covered what we are trying so hard to control.

God wants us to lean in and listen close as He says, *I've got this. Just like I've always had this. And by the way, I can do "immeasurably more than"* you could ever *"ask for or imagine"* **(EPH. 3:20)**. *Will you trust Me?*

Ponder your response to that invitation.

On a scale of 1 to 5, how difficult is it for you to trust God?

1   2   3   4   5

Did you notice what Jehoshaphat's motivation was to trust the Lord in such a profound way (see vv. 6-7)? It was in remembering the Lord's faithfulness in the past that empowered Jehoshaphat to trust the Lord for the future.

> What stories from Scripture, your life, or the lives of those around you remind you that God, not you, is the One holding all things together and can be trusted with your children?

God is our all-knowing, all-powerful, all-sufficient Father who gives us radical, extravagant, abundant grace.

CLOSE WITH PRAYER
Let's end today praising Him for who He is.

Our Sovereign Father, thank You for Your power and Your goodness. Like Paul, there are days when I am the worst of sinners. Forgive me for the times I doubt Your sovereignty and love. Help me to trust You with my heart, my life, and my kids. I will trust in Your grace. Like the psalmist, I will pray: "LORD, you are my portion and my cup of blessing; you hold my future. The boundary lines have fallen for me in pleasant places; indeed, I have a beautiful inheritance" **(PS. 16:5-6).**

DAY 4

Yesterday we explored the sovereignty of God, and today we will look at the grace of God. Not that these two things are independent from one another. They aren't. But it will help us further in our journey to have a common understanding of these words.

I can remember, so clearly, the first time I heard the expression, "Be the person you want your children to become." I had two children at the time, ages four and two, but my third was on the way. And I was a mess. Overwhelmed, discouraged, and disappointed in who I'd become—as my weaknesses and shortcomings were all being revealed and magnified through motherhood. So you can imagine the grief and despair I felt when I read an article urging me to be the person I wanted my children to become. Because, here's the thing—I thought that being the person I wanted them to become meant being perfect. I thought God was relying on me to be a perfect example for my kids to follow.

What emotions does the expression "be the person you want your children to become" evoke in you?

I know many moms who don't struggle with perfectionism but still feel the pressure of our culture's impossible standards to be close to flawless. How do you respond to that pressure? Are you more prone to try even harder, or does it make you just want to quit altogether? Explain.

What are the consequences of trying to be the perfect example for our kids to follow?

But we don't just feel the pressure from our culture. We might also think we find it in Scripture.

Read Titus 2:7. Write the verse in your own words.

Here, Paul was emphasizing to Titus that the example he set should foster rather than frustrate the spread of the gospel in the lives of people in Crete. Similarly, the example we set should foster rather than frustrate our children's understanding of what it looks like to follow Christ.

We must remember, though, our children don't need us to be the perfection of Christ. They need to see us in pursuit of Christ. They need us to point them to Christ. They need to see the power of Christ made perfect in our weaknesses.

We see this so beautifully demonstrated in Paul's own life.

Read 2 Corinthians 12:7-10. What was the affliction that Paul said was given to him (v. 7)?

Rather than respond to Paul's pleading by removing the affliction, what did God say to him? Answer by filling in the blank: "My _____ is all you need. My _____ works best in weakness" (v. 9, NLT).

Can we just sit with that for a minute? We will get to how Paul responded in a moment, but first can we put ourselves in Paul's shoes and think about how we'd respond to God's answer?

Share how you think you might have responded to God's answer.

I'm pretty confident I would have said something along the lines of, *God, thank You for Your grace. I appreciate that. I really do. But I don't think You heard me right. I don't want affliction. I don't like feeling weak. I want to be awesome. I want to be strong. I want to be self-sufficient and perfect. I guess what I'm saying, Lord, is that I don't want to need You or have to rely on Your power. I'd rather be You.*

Now let's look at how Paul responds in verses 9-10:

"So now I am glad to _____ about my _____, so that the power of Christ can _____" (NLT).

Paul shifted from begging God to remove his thorn to being glad to boast about the weaknesses it revealed—all at the mention of God's all-sufficient grace.

Grace is the unearned and undeserved favor of God.

Grace has no limits or conditions.

Grace is the means by which God saves, sustains, sanctifies, and strengthens us in the person and work of Jesus Christ.

Grace has no limits or conditions. In fact, grace with conditions isn't grace at all.

Scripture doesn't reveal the exact nature of Paul's thorn—whether it was physical, psychological, or situational. But Scripture does tell us what the thorn was intended to do.

Why was the thorn given to Paul?

And what is the opposite of pride or conceit?

The thorn was intended to keep Paul humble. Could it be that God loved Paul enough to give him the thorn to protect him from pride, to allow him to experience God's grace in profound ways, and to keep Paul reliant on God to provide everything he would need?

We all have thorns in our lives—different hardships or afflictions—that we experience. Ongoing marital strife, financial hardship, depression, addiction, physical pain or limitations, broken relationships with extended family, job insecurity, unfulfilled dreams, just to name a few. These thorns can bring us to our knees and reveal the greatness of our need.

> Have you seen God's grace proven all-sufficient and all-powerful in your weakness and need? If so, please explain.

Now let's apply this to our parenting. What hope does this passage give us as moms? See, the Lord's gracious assurance to Paul is the very same assurance He gives to you and to me. When we are striving but not succeeding at being flawless examples for our kids to follow, God says, "My grace is all you need. My power works best in weakness." So, just like the apostle Paul, we can boldly respond, *So now I can be glad to be honest with my children about my weaknesses, so that the divine power of Christ can work through me in my parenting. When I confess I am weak, I am finally strong.*

Our weaknesses

- help us parent from a posture of humility;

- keep us reliant on God to provide everything we need to parent the children He has entrusted to us; and

- allow us to experience for ourselves, and demonstrate to our kids, His sustaining grace.

Oh, the sweet relief I have found in knowing that my weaknesses point my children away from their flawed mom and straight to their flawless Savior. He's the One I want their trust and hope set upon, not me.

You don't have to be ashamed of your weaknesses and need. Jesus loves to meet you and equip you and strengthen you and glorify Himself through you in that place, by His grace. There is only One who has ever been a perfect example for our children to follow. And that One isn't us. It's Jesus.

Now this isn't to suggest that the example we set for our kids does not have a profound impact on them. Indeed it does. What we do and what we say absolutely matters. What we model has an enormous impact on the thought patterns and behavior of our children. I know you know the research. We should absolutely and wholeheartedly seek to be a godly example for them. But as hard as we try, we will fail. Confessing this does not make us failures; it makes us free—free to be moms who are honest about our weaknesses, grateful for our Savior, and eager to live in the likeness of Christ by the power of the Holy Spirit at work within us.

Did you catch the end of that sentence? We set an example not by relying on our own power but on the power of the Holy Spirit that is made perfect in our weakness. In light of this, I can actually get OK—even excited—about the expression "be the person you want them to become."

On a scale of 1-5, how free do you currently feel to be honest with your children about your weaknesses?

1   2   3   4   5

What has prevented you from feeling free to be honest? Or, what has enabled you to be honest?

What are some ways your life can demonstrate to your children that you are deeply grateful for how God's grace is sufficient for you?

How is striving to be a flawless example different than seeking to live in pursuit of Christ by the power of the Holy Spirit?

Paul says in **1 CORINTHIANS 11:1,** *"Imitate me, as I also imitate Christ."*

Who is the ultimate example that both Paul and the people of Corinth should have followed?

Paul encouraged the people of Corinth to imitate him because he sought to imitate Christ. As moms, we are to be an example to our children—but not an example of unachievable perfection. Instead, we strive to point them toward the One who is perfect for us as we follow His lead and rely on His Spirit.

Our goal does not need to be perfection but letting our children see us enjoying Him, and thereby glorifying Him, as we live the free and abundant life Christ came to give us.

CLOSE WITH PRAYER

Let's close today by thanking God for the gift of motherhood. And let us beg Him to help us remember and trust in His sovereignty and grace as we seek to lead and love our children to the praise and glory of His grace.

Write your own prayer of gratitude below.

What we do and what we say absolutely matters.

Every week on Day 5, we'll have a prayer activity to practice parenting open handed. Prayer is a powerful way to demonstrate our need for Christ and our reliance on Him for our kids. I may provide Scripture for you to meditate on, or a task I'll invite you to complete.

In 1 Peter 5:6-7, Peter told us to do two things. Humble ourselves and cast all of our anxiety on God. But it's "why" Peter told us to do this that always gets me. It's because God cares for us. My fellow mom, God cares so deeply for you. That means He cares about the things that you care about.

Casting our anxiety, worries, and problems on God is actually a very humbling act because it requires acknowledging that He is God and we are not. And it requires our trust in Him.

God is big enough and strong enough to bear the burdens and worries that are weighing you down. Will you join me now in casting it all on Him?

Today, we'll look at a few Scriptures that convey peace and repel worry. I hope you'll use these verses as prayers to our Father who is sovereign and full of grace.

> Look up one verse or a few and personalize them, making them into prayers to God for peace in the midst of worry and fear.

Psalm 5:3

Psalm 118:5-9

Proverbs 3:5-6

Isaiah 26:3-4

Philippians 4:6-7

We do our best parenting through prayer.

#MOMSETFREE

FREEDOM FROM THE PLACES WE GET STUCK

Group Discussion Questions

1. What was the most meaningful or significant thing you learned from this last week's study?

2. Where have you felt stuck because of the pressures you feel as a mom: worry, fear, anger, guilt, shame, comparison? What is the greatest struggle for you and why?

3. Read John 8:31-32. What happens when we abide in God's Word?

4. How might abiding in Scripture change our parenting and help us get out of the places where we get stuck?

5. When have you seen a difference in another mom and her parenting because of her relationship with Christ and walking with Him daily?

6. What is the greatest way we can encourage one another to trust God daily?

_____

_____

_____

_____

_____

_____

_____

To hear more from Jeannie, download the optional video bundle at lifeway.com/momsetfree

You came back for Week 2. Yay! I am so glad you're still here. No seriously, I am. I know how it is to start off a study motivated and excited, but to end up quickly sidelined by distractions and looming deadlines, or buried under dirty dishes, dirty diapers, and dirty laundry. So welcome back, warrior. This is going to be a great week.

We are pressing deeper into the specific pressures we ranked on Day 1 of last week. This week, my hope is that you will learn that whatever pressures you are facing as a mom, and whatever problems you are navigating alongside your children, you can do it with open hands and a trusting heart, realizing that God has called you to be an influencer and a nurturer, not a controller and an all-knower, in your children's lives.

I recently had dinner with a group of girlfriends who are also in the trenches of motherhood, and the ages of our children ranged from nine months to nineteen years old. This means our conversation reflected the concerns of a mom with a child who was just born, the concerns of a mom whose son had just finished rush at college, and everything in between. Have mercy. What stood out to me on this particular night was the vast and wide questions we were all grappling with and the enormity of the responsibility we all felt. *Should I force my child to go to church with us? Should I homeschool my kids or send them to private school or public school? Should they be allowed to play more than two sports? Should I let them go to the party on Friday night? Should I be worried that my child doesn't want to pray with us? Should I call the mother of the child who is torturing my kid in lacrosse? Should we visit five campuses or fifteen campuses before submitting college appli-cations? Should I let my child have a cell phone in sixth grade? Should I ... ? Should I ... ? Should I ...?* These are just a few of the important and heavy questions we ask as moms every day.

What are the parenting decisions you're grappling with in this season?

You know what is actually becoming more and more clear to me as I navigate the complexities of parenting a teenage boy, the physical exhaustion of parenting

a newborn son, and parenting two children in between? It's how God doesn't just work through us to grow our kids in His likeness. He works through them to grow us.

God grows us in holiness through the hardships of motherhood.

Now maybe you're thinking, *Really? Because I'm well aware of the hardships but I'm not seeing the "growing in holiness" part. In fact, all I see are my weaknesses, inadequacies, and sins being more and more exposed in my daily parenting and I am sinking deeper and deeper into despair.* If that's you, I get it. But sit tight because this week we will see how motherhood can indeed be sanctifying when we remember God's sovereignty and grace, and allow God to draw us closer in relationship to and reliance on Him.

Look at the words below. Circle the ones that reflect our parenting when we forget God's sovereignty and grace. Underline the words our parenting will be laced with when we remember God's sovereignty and grace.

worry	wonder	fear	anger
grace	love	pride	gentleness
shame	humility	guilt	compassion

One approach looks more like white knuckles gripping for control. One approach looks more like open hands ready to give and receive grace. And we don't have to look at those two lists for long to know which one is which and where we want to land.

On a scale of 1 to 5, 1 meaning "white knuckles" and 5 being "open handed," how would you say you parent on most days?

1   2   3   4   5

I know my answer to that question depends on what aspect of parenting we are discussing. For example, the area in which I tend to parent the most "white knuckled" is around my children's faith, as well as the fruit of their faith. And I have found that this is the area in which many Christian parents feel the most pressure. We so desperately want our children to know and love Jesus and to live Christlike lives. And that is a good and right thing to desire. More than anything else, that is what I desire. But it's when we actually start thinking we have the ability—as we said on Day 1—to create a saving and vibrant faith in our children's lives, or produce Christlike character in our children's lives, that we get into trouble. Ultimately this means we've bought into the falsehood that we have the power to control and transform our children's hearts.

There is good reason that so much emphasis is put on focusing on our children's hearts in our parenting. The heart is the center of a child's spirit, and everything the child does and says flows from it (Prov. 4:23; Luke 6:45).

But here's the important thing we have to remember when we focus on parenting our children's hearts. There is only One who can transform it. And that one isn't you or me. It is the Father, the Son, and the Holy Spirit. We can shepherd our children's hearts, but we are powerless to transform them.

How does that last sentence make you feel?

I have to admit, at first I saw this as very bad news. I didn't like feeling powerless. I wanted to get inside my kids' hearts and do some prioritizing and producing. I wanted to believe that if I put all the right stuff in, all the right stuff would come out. But it was only a matter of time before I realized that I can't manufacture faith or virtues in their lives any more than I can do that in my own. Rather, loving God and living in the likeness of Christ will be the manifestation of grace in their hearts, by the indwelling power of the Holy Spirit.

Let's explore some passages that speak directly to this.

> For no one can come to me unless the Father who sent me draws them
> to me, and at the last day I will raise them up.
> JOHN 6:44, NLT

The Lord does not delay his promise, as some understand delay, but is patient with you, not wanting any to perish but all to come to repentance.
2 PETER 3:9

Even before he made the world, God loved us and chose us in Christ to be holy and without fault in his eyes. God decided in advance to adopt us into his own family by bringing us to himself through Jesus Christ. This is what he wanted to do, and it gave him great pleasure.
EPHESIANS 1:4-5, NLT

What aspects of these verses bring comfort to you as you parent?

We can (and must) faithfully share the gospel (in word and deed) with our kids, but the Father must draw our children to His heart. We can't push and plead them there. Rather, He pursues them and woos them to Himself, and the Holy Spirit opens eyes to see and ears to hear Him.

Let us run with endurance the race that lies before us, keeping our eyes on Jesus, the source and perfecter of our faith. For the joy that lay before him, he endured the cross, despising the shame, and sat down at the right hand of the throne of God.
HEBREWS 12:1b-2

Who is the source and perfecter of your children's faith? What does that mean for your role as their mom?

So we can't produce a thriving faith, but we can partner with God by planting seeds of faith.

Read 1 Corinthians 3:6-7. What is our role in our children's salvation?

What is God's role?

How do you plant and water seeds of faith in your child's life?

How do these verses empower you to parent more open-handed when teaching your kids the gospel and seeking to nurture their faith?

Let's look at a few passages about the pressure we feel to produce Christlike character in our children's lives.

We are dependent upon God to shape us into the likeness of His Son.

I am certain that God, who began the good work within you, will continue his work until it is finally finished on the day when Christ Jesus returns. … I pray that your love will overflow more and more, and that you will keep on growing in knowledge and understanding. For I want you to understand what really matters, so that you may live pure and blameless lives until the day of Christ's return. May you always be filled with the fruit of your salvation—the righteous character produced in your life by Jesus Christ—for this will bring much glory and praise to God.
PHILIPPIANS 1:6,9-11, NLT

Who began the good work?

How long will He continue His work?

Who produces righteous character in our lives?

And this will bring much praise to our parenting or to God?

Now read Isaiah 64:8. Who sits on the potter's stool?

Just as clay is dependent upon the potter to be shaped, so are we dependent upon God to shape us into the likeness of His Son.

> *For it is God who is working in you both to will and to work according to his good purpose.*
> PHILIPPIANS 2:13

Note the two things Philippians 2:13 says God gives to us and to our children. The NLT translation says God gives both "the desire and the power to do what pleases him." And He does this by His grace. This is no small thing.

Now here's what embracing this truth does. It inclines us to take a good, long look at the significance of our role in our children's lives in light of God's sovereignty over their lives. And, hopefully, it ultimately inclines us to surrender our children's faith, and the fruit of that faith, into the hands of our all-powerful and all-loving God.

Friend, we want to be open-handed and wide-eyed to the wonder and adventure of parenting. And the good news is, we can! We can live—and parent—freely and lightly in the assurance of God's sovereignty and grace. We've only just begun our journey to parenting as moms set free. I am so grateful for the gift of traveling alongside you.

I believe, with all my heart, that God has you doing this study for a reason. The fact that you are holding this study in your hands is not an accident or a coincidence. It is God's providence. He made you a mother. And He wants to give you everything you need to be the mom you long to be for the children He entrusted to you.

CLOSE WITH PRAYER
Let's close today by praying Psalm 139:1-5. Write your thoughts after reading these verses and allow God to remind you that He knows your every need.

One of my boys recently endured a very difficult experience at school in which he was being targeted by another student. It was unbearably painful to send my son to school each day knowing the circumstances he would likely have to navigate as we worked to ensure the situation was properly addressed and resolved. Oh, my mama bear instincts were in full force. But I also had to remember that this is part of growing up in a fallen world, and the best thing I could do for him was equip him for the hardship, walk beside him through it, and point to God's presence in it, rather than simply scoop him out of it.

This is another area in which we feel immense pressure—protecting our children from hardship and/or suffering. There is a profound difference in helping our kids navigate hardship and providing comfort in their suffering versus feeling guilty that we cannot completely protect them from it.

Today we will also touch on the pressure we feel to ensure our children fulfill their full potential and purpose. Goodness, I sure would love to ensure they do. I know you would too. We love these kids and want so much for them, and it is painful to watch them waste their gifts, choose the path of destruction, or doubt the fact that God made them for a beautiful purpose. If I've learned anything in this last year, it's that we can (and should) cast a vision for our children. We give our children an extraordinary gift by teaching them that God made them on purpose, for a specific purpose, with unique giftings to fulfill their calling, all for the praise of His name. But just because we cast a vision doesn't mean we can make them catch it.

READ ROMANS 8:28-32:

28 We know that all things work together for the good of those who love God, who are called according to his purpose. 29 For those he foreknew he also predestined to be conformed to the image of his Son, so that he would be the firstborn among many brothers and sisters. 30 And those he predestined, he also called; and those he called, he also justified; and those he justified, he also glorified. 31 What then are we to say about these things? If God is for us, who is against us? 32 He did not even spare his own Son but offered him up for us all. How will he not also with him grant us everything?

This passage can provide us much comfort as parents, but it can also create great confusion, which is why whole books have been written on it and entire sermon series have been devoted to it. So I'm not going to attempt to completely unpack it here. Rather my intent is to give us a glimpse of the sovereignty of our good Father. And my hope is that we will ultimately see this passage as an invitation to take a long, deep breath of relief.

It's important to remember, God has given all of us free will. We are all responsible for the choices we make. Indeed, our choices matter. However, God is not limited by our choices. He is continually working everything according to His plan and His purpose. We may not always understand God's plan, but we have to trust that He is working things for our good and His glory.

Here are a few encouraging truths that we can take away from this passage for our parenting, when we see our kids enduring hardship or suffering.

- God is loving—extraordinarily loving (Deut. 7:9; Ps. 86:15; 1 John 3:16).

- God is not the author of evil in our kids' lives (Deut. 32:4; Jas. 1:17).

- God is present in our children's pain, as close as the air they breathe (Ps. 34:18; 56:8; 2 Cor. 1:3-5).

   So then what is the good toward which God is working that Paul wrote about in Romans 8:28-32? (Hint: look at vv. 29-30.)

God's good plan for our children is to draw their hearts closer to His and conform them into the likeness of His Son. What more could we want for our children?

Watching God grow our children in the likeness of Christ—also known as sanctification—will rarely be pain-free. It will even break our hearts at times. Believers are not exempt from suffering. In fact, Scripture is clear, we should expect it. But as we expectantly wait for that day when God will make everything as it should be, let us not lose sight of the privilege we have in being part of God's overall redemptive narrative. We can have full confidence that He is still on the throne and He knows exactly what He is doing. He goes with our children, He is for our children, and somehow, someway, He is working all things together *"for the good of those who love God, who are called according to his purpose"* **(v. 28).**[1]

This passage has often been used to deduce that God works all things together for your own personal good, no matter who you are and regardless of how painful those things are, but *good* in this passage does not equal *good* in the way the world describes it. Good outcomes might eventually arise from the bad, but that is not ultimately the good that God's pursuing and Paul spoke of here.

The good, as Paul wrote, is conforming us more and more into the image of Jesus.

The good is so much greater than how we tend to think of it. So we, as parents, can have confidence that God is going to bring a new heaven and new earth. When that happens there will be no more pain, no more brokenness, and all things will be restored—but He has not put a time frame on that. We will not always see how our child's circumstances are redeemed in the greater narrative of redemption.

> Reread verse 32, and reflect on how God has already proven Himself so good and generous. Record your thoughts below.

> How does this truth give you hope for your children's struggles?

Though we can't fix all their pain, we can be present in it. When our kids are hurting, crushed, or confused, they need parents who are willing to lean into their pain, listen without lecturing, and love without limits.

We can also find extraordinary peace in Scripture that assures us that our suffering does not have the final word—and that all of this heartache and hurt will ultimately produce a hope that will not disappoint because we will share in the glory of Christ.

We find this assurance again in Paul's writing on suffering in Romans 5:

> *Not only that, but we rejoice in our sufferings, knowing that suffering produces endurance, and endurance produces character, and character produces hope, and hope does not put us to shame, because God's love has been poured into our hearts through the Holy Spirit who has been given to us.*
> ROMANS 5:3-5, ESV

Note the progression here:

suffering $\longrightarrow$ _____ $\longrightarrow$ character $\longrightarrow$ _____

And hope does not disappoint.

Note that Paul says we can "rejoice in"—not *because of*, but *in*—our problems and trials because of what they produce in us. The happiness or ease that we want for our children is rarely the path to perseverance, character, and ultimately hope—a hope anchored in how very much we can trust that God loves us and is for us, even in our suffering.

Let's not forget, our children were God's good idea to begin with. Your son. Your daughter. They were God's good idea. They are His workmanship.

To close today, I want to look at one more verse about God's plan for our children.

Read Proverbs 22:6. Please write it below.

How has this passage influenced your parenting? Have you read this passage as a proverb or a promise?

My hope is that we will see this proverb, which tends to put some pressure on moms, as an invitation to open-handed parenting. But to do that, we have to distinguish the difference in a proverb and a promise.

If we read this proverb as an if-then promise—if we train up our children correctly, then they will not turn away from our teaching—we will parent under pressure, thinking our child's future is riding solely on our performance. Our mentality is either, *It's all about me, and if I get it mostly right, my kids will stay on the right path*, or *It's all about me, and if I get it mostly wrong, my kids will turn down the wrong path.*

But if we read this proverb for what it is—wisdom for godly living—we will see this passage as an invitation to identify and develop the unique personality, disposition, and giftedness that God has hidden in our child, to His glory, not ours. And ultimately, it will lead us to trust Him with the fruit of our labor.

Identify a few of the ways God has gifted your children and think about how to point them to use those gifts for His glory.

We hold profound significance in our children's lives, but we are not sovereign.

Rather than be ruled by worry, we can parent in wonder—hopeful curiosity and expectation—of what God is doing in the lives of our kids. Rather than be ruled by fear, we can parent by faith, showing *"the reality of what we hope for; it is the evidence of things we cannot see"* **(HEB. 11:1, NLT).**

Pray, and ask God to help you parent with open hands.

CLOSE WITH PRAYER
Lord, thank You for the hope of salvation. Make my faith in You stronger than my fears. Help me to trust You more with every part of my life, but especially my parenting. Help me to be faithful to train up my children in the truth of Your Word.

DAY 3

I need to start today by confessing something to you. More than anything else I have shared with you in this study, this is by far the most convicting to me personally. Because today we are going to talk about the power of prayer in our parenting. But you need to know, my default is problem-solving, not praying. I'm a problem solver. That's what I do. So nobody needs to be reminded of this more than me: we do our best parenting through prayer.

Oswald Chambers, in *My Utmost For His Highest,* said "Prayer is the practice of drawing on the grace of God. Don't say, 'I will endure this until I can get away and pray.' Pray *now*—draw on the grace of God in your moment of need. Prayer is the most normal and useful thing; it is not simply a reflex action of your devotion to God. We are very slow to learn to draw on God's grace through prayer."[2]

Prayer is the most powerful thing we can do for our kids.

Our children need us to be prayer warriors before they need us to be problem-solvers.

Do you believe your prayers matter to God? Why or why not?

How have you seen your prayers impact your child's life?

What keeps you from praying for your children more?

Prayer gives us inexhaustible access to God's peace and God's power, both of which we desperately need in our mothering.

Read Philippians 4:6-7, and summarize the verses in your own words:

What has Paul told us to do instead of worry?

What did Paul tell us to pray about in verse 6?

What does Paul say we will experience as a result of prayer?

Maybe you're a mom who doesn't know how to pray or what to say. Or perhaps you're in a season where you feel particularly helpless or hopeless. Or maybe words fail you because you are so overwhelmed and under pressure that you don't even know where to begin. Or you're worried that your doubts or lack of faith will hinder your prayers for your children. Well, I have more encouraging news for you.

READ ROMANS 8:26-28 (MSG):
Meanwhile, the moment we get tired in the waiting, God's Spirit is right alongside helping us along. If we don't know how or what to pray, it doesn't matter. He does our praying in and for us, making prayer out of our wordless sighs, our aching groans. He knows us far better than we know ourselves, knows our pregnant condition, and keeps us present before God. That's why we can be so sure that every detail in our lives of love for God is worked into something good.

The assurance Paul gave us in Romans 8 is that God's very Spirit—who knows us better than we know ourselves—takes our cries for help and prays for us. That's incredible. If you've ever felt pressure to get it all right in prayer, fear no more. Run to Him. Be honest with Him. Share your heart with Him. You don't have to know exactly what to say or how to say it. He isn't judging or critiquing your prayers. Nobody listens better than Jesus.

READ JAMES 1:5:
Now if any of you lacks wisdom, he should ask God—who gives to all generously and ungrudgingly—and it will be given to him.

How often do you feel like you don't know what you're doing as a parent?

What did James tell us to do?

What did James tell us the Father does?

We are invited to bring all of our worries, fears, burdens, and pressures to our all-knowing and all-loving Father who loves to help. So what in the world are we doing settling for anything less than that?

READ PSALM 118:5-9 (ESV):
5 Out of my distress I called on the LORD; the LORD answered me and set me free. 6 The LORD is on my side; I will not fear. What can man do to me? 7 The LORD is on my side as my helper; I shall look in triumph on those who hate me. 8 It is better to take refuge in the LORD than to trust in man. 9 It is better to take refuge in the LORD than to trust in princes.

Write verse 5 below.

What did the psalmist promise us the Lord would do in verses 5 and 7?

Call to God. His peace and His power are for you, and they are for right now.

That's right, friend. *Set you free.*

Call to God. His peace and His power are for you, and they are for right now.

Our prayers for our children (and with our children) are unimaginably significant. Through prayer, we get to partner with God in the work He is doing in the lives of our kids, all the while remembering that, *"It won't be long before this generous God who has great plans for us in Christ—eternal and glorious plans they are!—will have you put together and on your feet for good. He gets the last word; yes, he does"* **(1 PET. 5:10-11, MSG).**

Now, this is not discounting the fact that there are very real things we must do and very difficult problems we must solve. Nowhere in Scripture do we read, "Pray only." Right? But we are continually reminded that this is the best place to start and the best place to return. As we navigate each one of the pressures we've covered, and we do the things God has called us to do as parents, we can do it with open hands and trusting hearts—believing that God is sovereign, that He is good, and that there is grace upon grace for us and for our kids.

Open-handed is the best way to approach our paramount purpose as parents. We'll talk more in-depth on that tomorrow!

CLOSE WITH PRAYER
JAMES 1:6 tells us, *"But let him ask in faith without doubting."* Pray boldly, believing that God will hear your prayers.

DAY 4

We're on our last day of looking at the specific pressures we are under as parents, and my prayer is that we are slowly but surely moving from gripping for control to trusting the One who is sovereign over it all. Carrying a much lighter load, we are empowered to thrive in our paramount purpose as parents. We have a lot of good ground to cover today, so I want to get right to it.

READ DEUTERONOMY 6:4-7 (NIV):
Hear, O Israel: The LORD our God, the LORD is one. Love the LORD your God with all your heart and with all your soul and with all your strength. These commandments that I give you today are to be on your hearts. Impress them on your children. Talk about them when you sit at home and when you walk along the road, when you lie down and when you get up.

Let's not miss how Moses affirmed God's sovereignty before he conveyed God's teaching on our significant role as parents.

What is the first command God gives us in this passage?

What are we told to do with God's commandments?

READ MATTHEW 22:35-40 (NIV):
One of them, an expert in the law, tested him with this question: "Teacher, which is the greatest commandment in the Law?" Jesus replied: "'Love the Lord your God with all your heart and with all your soul and with all your mind.' This is the first and greatest commandment. And the second is like it: 'Love your neighbor as yourself.' All the Law and the Prophets hang on these two commandments."

Indeed, Christ's words echo Moses' many centuries later. What is the common theme between these two passages?

Seeking to raise children who love the Lord with all their hearts, souls, and minds is our highest calling as parents.

Read 1 John 4:19. Why do we love?

God's love for us inspires our love for Him.

What does this gospel message have to do with our parenting? Everything! Because within the gospel we discover how to fulfill our calling. Our children's love for God will be their grateful response to the love God has given them in the sacrifice of His Son. God's love for us inspires our love for Him.

We impress on our kids a whole-being love for God by first impressing on our kids God's indescribable love for them.

See, our kids need to know God's heart for them before they will ever desire to seek His heart above all else. They need to know the extent to which God went to rescue them and demonstrate His love for them in the life, death, and resurrection of Jesus Christ.

He made the one who did not know sin to be sin for us, so that in him we might become the righteousness of God.
2 CORINTHIANS 5:21

If we try to raise kids who love God by only giving them the commandments of God and telling them they should love God, then we'll more likely raise rule-followers than God-lovers. We'll more likely raise kids who flee the faith, because rules don't breed gratitude and melt our hearts. Love does.

Apply this in your own life. Is it the shoulds and oughts that have inspired you to love God and walk in obedience to Him? Or is it that He pursued you, poured out His life for you, and purchased your freedom while you were still running and rebelling?

Reflect on your own experience. Journal how it has impacted your walk with God.

Friend, of all the things we want to give our kids, let us not lose sight of the one thing that matters above all else: giving them the gospel.

The gospel is the good news that Jesus' perfect life, death, and resurrection has secured God's eternal and unwavering love for us, acceptance of us, delight in us, and pleasure over us. We never have to fear our Father's rejection. We can never out-sin His grace. We can never lose His love (see Eph. 2:4-5).

We have the great privilege and responsibility of impressing upon our kids this heart-melting, life-giving news.

Indeed, it is both a privilege and a responsibility. And trust me when I tell you, I'm talking to myself here because I am often convicted about how I prioritize nurturing my child's faith. I have to re-evaluate continually what I prioritize in our lives and whether I am parenting with eternity in the forefront of my mind.

Identify what you most want for your children.

Go back through that list and prioritize those things.

What is God's desire for our children?

If your desires don't align with God's, why do you think that is?

Where does discipleship land in our priorities—not just in word but in deed?

Our culture tells us that our ultimate goal should be to launch kids who will have big bank accounts and big resumes and big awards and big toys. But Scripture paints a very different picture. Our ultimate goal should be to launch kids who have a big faith anchored in the big grace of God. Of all the things we can give our kids in this world, God has called us to give them Him above all else. Because only in Him will they find the fulfillment their hearts crave, and only in Him will they find the purpose-filled future He designed for them. This world is not their permanent home, and it's our job to help them live in light of eternity—living in the grace of God for the glory of God.

That being said, I want to assure you that I have never (and I mean never) met a parent who feels like they're doing enough to disciple their kids. The mom whose kids memorized the entire Book of James, and the mom who has never done any Scripture memory can both feel like they aren't doing enough. And the enemy uses this to make us give up altogether.

Instead of giving up or living with guilt, can we identify places where we can make changes?

In Weeks 5 and 6, we will get to the very practical and daily ways we can make the gospel central in our homes. Rest assured you will be empowered and equipped to parent from purpose rather than pressure by the end of our journey. But before we go there, we have to go here—to our own hearts.

Friend, I couldn't wait for us to get to this part.

See, if you're anything like me, you're chomping at the bit for the practical ways you can parent as a mom set free.

But first, we need to know—really know—that Jesus loves us and that His grace is for us. We need to allow God to do in us what we ultimately long for Him to do in our children—to melt our hearts with His love and mold us more and more into His image by the power of His Holy Spirit.

This, my friend, is how we will become more of the moms we long to be for our kids. Not by trying harder but by more deeply believing the gospel for ourselves. All the pressure we've been carrying—the pressure to be awesome for God, the pressure to be awesome for our kids, and the pressure to raise awesome kids—we can lay it all down.

CLOSE WITH PRAYER

Pray with great expectation that God is about to transform your heart with His wild love. Pray that He will free you to live—and parent—in the fullness of His grace.

There are a lot of places where we can find ourselves stuck in our parenting. But one of the greatest hindrances to parenting is fear. Fear that we will mess up. Fear that we will make the wrong choice. Fear that our children's negative behaviors reflect upon our lack of parenting skills. Fear that our kids will be totally ruined because we just don't know what we are doing.

Parenting out of fear causes us to withhold grace.

Read these verses and record your thoughts.

Isaiah 41:10

John 14:27

1 Peter 3:13-15

How do these verses bring you hope as you face your fears?

Read 2 Corinthians 9:8. What is God able to do?

What is the "so that" of this verse?

What is the one "next thing" you can do to make giving the gospel to your children your top priority?

CLOSE WITH PRAYER

Write your prayers to God today. Unload the fears you have for yourself and your children. Ask God to make His grace overflow through you.

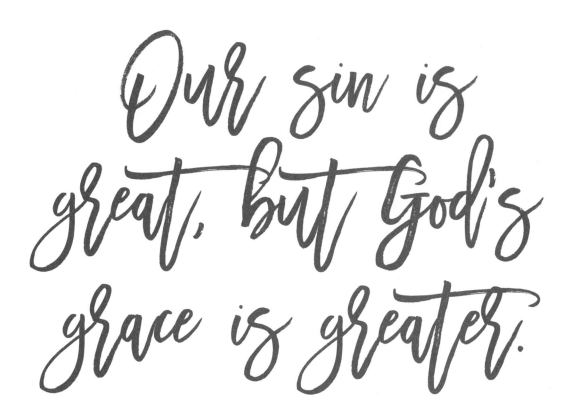

Our sin is great, but God's grace is greater.

#MOMSETFREE

FREEDOM TO RECEIVE THE LOVE OF JESUS

Group Discussion Questions

1. How did God speak to you most through last week's study?

2. Where do you find strength for your parenting?

3. How does prayer impact you? How are you finding power in prayer?

4. What do you think is God's greatest purpose for you as a mom?

5. What do you believe God wants most for your children? Why?

6. Read Ephesians 2:8-9. God's grace is for our salvation and our ongoing sin. What does it mean to be a grace-full parent?

7. How can you demonstrate unconditional love to your children this week? How can you assure them of your love, full of grace and acceptance?

_____

_____

_____

_____

_____

_____

_____

_____

To hear more from Jeannie,
download the optional video
bundle at lifeway.com/momsetfree

Becoming the grace-full parent we long to be will happen to the extent that we allow the grace of God to fill our own hearts. But this is no easy thing. I think Martin Luther was onto something when he said, "It is the hardest thing that can be, to be certainly persuaded in our hearts, that by grace alone (all other means in heaven or in earth set apart) we have remission [forgiveness] of sins and peace with God."[1]

We have to trust the Word of God over the merciless critic in our heads.

Our ability to lead our children in the love of Christ is profoundly influenced by our acceptance of how Jesus loves us. And not just the lovable parts of us but all of us, all of the time. Not just when we are obeying Him, trusting Him, and pulling this parenting thing off pretty well. But when we are messing up again, losing our patience again, being unthankful again, doing that "thing" we were determined to stop doing again. On the days when we don't feel the least bit lovely or lovable, we remain His beloved. We have to trust the Word of God over the merciless critic in our heads. We must make every untrue and rebellious *"thought captive to obey Christ"* (**2 COR. 10:5**).

And I can't think of a passage where this is more beautifully displayed than in the story Jesus told, as recorded in the Gospel of Luke, chapter 15, about the lost son.

Jesus told the crowd about a rebellious son who demands his inheritance from his father, sets off to satisfy his every desire, squanders his inheritance, and—after losing everything and finding himself in the depths of despair—returns home to his father.

But to the son's amazement, the father—the father he demanded his inheritance from, the father whose heart he shattered—graciously and gladly welcomes his son home.

Luke describes the son's return this way: *"So he got up and went to his father. But while the son was still a long way off, his father saw him and was filled with compassion. He ran, threw his arms around his neck, and kissed him"* **(LUKE 15:20).**

He ran to his rebellious son. Before his son ever spoke one word of regret or remorse or apology, the father ran to his son and embraced him.

The unconditional love and absolute acceptance the father had for his son in this parable symbolizes the unconditional love and absolute acceptance our heavenly Father has for us. God's love for us isn't just for our salvation—it covers our ongoing sin, failure, and rebellion.

Because of Jesus, we never have to fear our Father's rejection. We can never out-sin His grace. We can never lose His love.

Jesus told this story to show us what God's love is like. So that we would walk in freedom. So that we wouldn't waste our time fearing His rejection and trying to earn back His love and forgiveness when we sin, but rather that we would run to Him, repent, and believe the good news that Jesus loves and welcomes sinners.

What does any of this have to do with parenting?

Before we can give grace and show grace to our children—before we can lead them in knowing, experiencing, and enjoying the unconditional love of God—we first need to accept and enjoy the grace God has freely given us in Christ Jesus. We have to receive God's acceptance of us—in all of our parenting mistakes, failures, and weaknesses. We can't give what we haven't received.

> Read Colossians 1:3-23. Now let's unpack it.

SCRIPTURE	ANSWERS
Colossians 1:6 What does the good news do?	
Colossians 1:9-10 How do we grow?	

SCRIPTURE	ANSWERS
Colossians 1:11 What gives us strength?	
Colossians 1:15-18 What do these verses tell us about Christ?	
Colossians 1:19-22 What truths are taught in these verses?	

As moms, we want to honor and please the Lord. We want our lives to *"produce every kind of good fruit"* **(v. 10, NLT).** But we are prone to think that the way this happens is by us trying harder and harder. Of course we have to invest in our relationships with God. We have to put in the time and effort, like in any relationship that we want to grow. But growth happens by coming to know God better, not by trying harder to please Him.

God gives us His "glorious power"—not our own—for the patience and endurance we need as moms. And Jesus purchased our freedom and forgave our sins. God reconciled us to Himself.

Read Colossians 1:23.

This verse is a beautiful charge to moms to believe the good news, stand firmly in it, and not drift away from the assurance of it.

Believing you are unconditionally loved by God is not a truth you master or have to fully understand before you lead your children in believing it. Grace can't be mastered. Instead, we can discover, receive, and enjoy God's grace alongside our kids. None of us will ever fully wrap our heads around it. In fact, the older I get the more aware I become of just how much I still have to discover about God's grace and how much God uses my kids to teach me about His grace. Amen? Amen!

CLOSE WITH PRAYER
Lord, I need Your grace. I need to experience it for myself and share Your grace with others. Thank You for welcoming me back to You again and again.

DAY 2

When we are in Christ, God will never stop loving us, because *"God is love"* **(1 JOHN 4:8).** He loves the real and imperfect us. But believing this truth can be so hard. There are simply too many parts of us that feel unworthy and unlovable.

This kind of grace, this inexhaustible love of God, goes against every other reality in our lives.

The world tells us, a little more perfect equals a little more lovable. So we think *the more perfect I can be, the more lovable I will be.* Then, we mistakenly take that equation and apply it to our relationship with our heavenly Father. We falsely think *the better I can be for God, the more I will be loved and accepted by Him.*

> When and how have you struggled with this false equation that perfect equals lovable in your relationships with others and with God?

The truth is that God created us to thrive in the unwavering assurance of His love given to us because of Jesus. However, what most of us are doing would not be considered thriving but something radically different. Instead of thriving in God's love, we are striving for something that is actually already all ours. And oftentimes we are unaware and don't even realize we are living this way.

With our mouths we will say, "I know God loves me." But the way we live our lives—ceaselessly striving and trying harder to be better to earn or keep His love and affection—tells a different story.

I speak from experience on this one! I was raised as a preacher's kid in a very grace-filled home. So when God saved me when I was eight years old, I understood, as much as an eight year old can understand, that *"For you are saved by grace through faith, and this is not from yourselves; it is God's gift—not from works, so that no one can boast"* **(EPH. 2:8-9).**

But what I struggled to accept was that God's grace was not just for my salvation but for my ongoing sin and weakness. So the older I got, and the more my sinful nature was exposed, and the more opportunities I had to mess up and *"fall short of the glory of God"* **(ROM. 3:23),** the more I struggled to accept the ongoing unconditional love of God for me, and the more pressure I felt to attain unachievable perfection.

I was trying hard to earn love from God through my good behavior for God. I didn't realize the profound implications of grace for my ongoing sinfulness and need.

> *He made the one who did not know sin to be sin for us, so that in him we might become the righteousness of God.*
> 2 CORINTHIANS 5:21

Author and pastor Beau Hughes explains, "Athanasius, the early church father in the fourth century, called this the glorious exchange, that Christ, the Son of God, got the punishment and took the punishment of an enemy of God so we, who are enemies of God, could receive the blessings of sons and daughters of God. It's the glorious exchange. Believing in this, putting your hope in this, and living by this, is at the heart of what it means to be a Christian."[2] Quite glorious, indeed.

Look at the exchange:

God takes our _____.

He gives us His _____.

When we are in Christ, we are covered in *"the righteousness of God"* **(2 COR. 5:21).** Jesus did for us what we could never do for ourselves. If we could be enough and do enough, it's as if *"Christ died for nothing"* **(GAL. 2:21).**

S.S.S. GRACE
By grace, we are saved, sanctified, and strengthened.

Begin with defining *grace* in your own words.

Grace is God's unmerited favor and undeserved love toward us because of the atoning sacrifice and finished work of His Son, Jesus Christ. Grace persists when we resist. Grace pursues us in our most unlovable moments. Grace is a love that knows the depths of your heart and loves you just the same. Grace is God's unending acceptance of you and unrestrained affection for you. If grace came with conditions or exceptions or strings attached, then *"grace ceases to be grace"* **(ROM. 11:6b).**

We are saved by grace.

What do the following verses teach us about grace?

Ephesians 2:8-9

2 Timothy 1:8-9

Titus 3:4-7

Jesus has saved us and called us to a holy life. This is not because of anything we have done (good or bad), but because of His own purpose and grace. God saves us by His grace and empowers us to pursue a holy life. But this is not a free pass to do as we please. We pursue holiness in response to God's love, not to earn God's love. We pursue holiness because we are God's beloved, not to become His beloved.

We are sanctified by grace.

Sanctification may not be a word we often hear, but it's important to unpack and understand if we want to live in freedom. *Sanctification* is the ongoing process of growing in the likeness of Christ through the power of the Holy Spirit.

Define *sanctification* in your own words.
(Look it up in the dictionary if you need to.)

We pursue holiness in response to God's love, not to earn God's love.

I like to think of sanctification as our ongoing growth in grace. This is an important distinction because we tend to think of sanctification as "trying harder to get better" in our own power, which could make us think we need the power of the Holy Spirit less and less. We figure if we just think the right things and do the right things, then we will work our way closer to holiness and keep God happy with us.

But growing in the likeness of Christ can't be done in our own will or effort. We grow spiritually when our hearts are melted and motivated by the good news of the gospel. Meaning, obedience that God wants is obedience that is the overflow of a grateful heart—a heart that is grateful for the grace God has shown us in Jesus Christ. Author Dennis Johnson further explains sanctification in his book, *Him We Proclaim:*

> Christians are constantly tempted to relapse into legalistic attitudes in their pursuit of sanctification, so we never outgrow our need to hear the good news of God's free and sovereign grace in Christ. Sanctification, no less than justification, must come by grace alone, through faith alone—we grow more like Christ only by growing more consistent in trusting Christ alone, thinking, feeling, acting *"in line with the truth of the gospel"* **(GAL. 2:14, ESV).** From this grace alone can flow true sanctification, motivated by gratitude and empowered by the Spirit.[3]

Read these verses, and then record how they might impact your parenting.

John 1:16

Romans 5:20-21

2 Thessalonians 2:13

God's grace and His desire for us is to live a life full of grace and gratefulness.

What does living full of His abundant grace mean for your life?
For your parenting?

There is always more grace. Unlimited grace. Inexhaustible grace. Grace upon grace.

We are strengthened by grace.

God's power shines through our weakness. But His grace also empowers us and strengthens us in our weakness.

Read Paul's words to Timothy:

You, therefore, my son, be strong in the grace that is in Christ Jesus.
2 TIMOTHY 2:1

Paul wrote to Timothy, his spiritual son in the faith, encouraging him to be strong in the grace that is in Christ Jesus. Grace is a continual source of power in a mother's life.

In what area(s) of your parenting do you feel especially weak right now?

What would relying on the power of Christ look like in the areas where you feel the most weak right now?

When we rely on Christ and the power of His Holy Spirit, we honor Him. We give God the praise and glory due to Him.

CLOSE WITH PRAYER

Father, thank You for Your perfect grace. Thank You for saving me, sanctifying me, and strengthening me. Help me to rely on You and Your grace as I parent. Amen.

DAY 3

Yesterday, we explored the amazing grace of God. We know that our sin is great, but God's grace is greater!

Still, there are days when all I see are the mistakes, the misses, and the failures as a mom and as a person. My heart wrestles with the truth of what I know God wants for me as His daughter in Christ.

> Read Romans 7:18-24, and describe Paul's angst.

> Can you relate? Which phrases resonate with you most as a mom?

> Now let's read Romans 7:24-25, and see the relief Paul experienced. What was the answer to the question in verse 24?

The answer is Jesus! Paul described his mind as being under the authority of God. Here, he was reminded that Jesus Christ is the One who had rescued him. Paul showed us that he was painfully aware of who he was in the flesh—in his persistent, sinful, broken nature—and yet, at the very same time, his assurance and his hope were in his identity in Christ.

As moms, one of the greatest challenges we face is the condemning thoughts that go through our minds. We can become consumed with our mistakes or the misses in our parenting and forget about the grace of God. But God wants us to remember grace upon grace.

> Read Romans 8:1. What does this verse promise?

"No condemnation." Not a little. None. So while *"we are no longer slaves to sin"* **(ROM. 6:6, NLT),** our battle with sin isn't gone when we are in Christ. Rather, Paul wrote, *"I am no longer the one doing it, but it is sin living in me"* **(ROM. 7:17).** Paul had separated his identity as a child of God from the sin that remained within him.

I love how Tim Keller has framed this. He writes, "We are more sinful and flawed in ourselves than we ever dared believe, yet at the very same time we are more loved and accepted in Jesus Christ than we ever dared hope."[4]

Keller's words have had a profound impact on my life because they revealed that the Christian life is not either/or. It's both/and. God, who sees into the deep recesses of our hearts, welcomes us at our very worst. And by His grace, He changes our identities from rebellious sinner to radically loved friend of God.

> READ ROMANS 8:38-39:
> *For I am persuaded that neither death nor life, nor angels nor rulers, nor things present nor things to come, nor powers, nor height nor depth, nor any other created thing will be able to separate us from the love of God that is in Christ Jesus our Lord.*

> List the things that cannot separate us from God's love.

And yet, how many of us read those verses and think there is surely something we bring to the cross that falls under the "everything but that" category of God's love. We read, "nothing but _____ can separate me from the love of God."

Can we get uncomfortable for a moment? Can we pause here and be honest with ourselves about those small and big things we put on that "nothing but _____" line?

> These are just a few of the regrets, mistakes, and sins we tend to think put a wall between us and God. Please circle those you relate to.

my past	temper	pride	anger
an eating disorder	an affair	an abortion	financial problems
an addiction	divorce	lies	jealousy
lack of gratitude	impatience	apathy	poor parenting

What other things have you been holding onto that you fear have built a wall between you and God's love?

I realize this might be a painful exercise, especially if you're still feeling the sting of sin and carrying shame. We don't see ourselves through God's lens of mercy and grace. Instead, we see ourselves exactly as the enemy would have us see ourselves—through the lens of condemnation and shame.

Our sin and rebellion do break the heart of God. But because of Jesus our sin and rebellion do not make us less lovable to Him. Because of Jesus, we are hidden in Christ; all God sees is the righteousness of His Son covering us (see Rom. 5:9-11).

His grace is big enough.

So friend, I need you to know this. Whatever it is that you insert on that "nothing but _____" line, His grace is big enough.

The cross outweighs all of our offenses. The big ones. The little ones. And all the in-between ones. So we are free to get honest with ourselves about ourselves, and we are free to get honest with one another about whatever it is that makes us feel we are unworthy of God's affection and unwelcome at His table.

Jesus doesn't offer us a "nothing but _____" kind of love. His is an "even that" kind of love. So let's beg God to help us believe that's true so we can live in freedom from shame.

CLOSE WITH PRAYER
Heavenly Father, I praise You for Your Son. Thank You for loving me. Thank You for forgiving me. Help me to live and parent as one forgiven. Amen.

DAY 4

Friend, we've been digging deep and unearthing regrets and sins and mistakes that we might be tempted to think are better kept buried. My prayer today is that we will encounter the deep love of Jesus and allow Him to free us from the shame we've carried for far too long.

Today is very personal because I am well-acquainted with shame. For so much of my life my mind-set was, "You paid the price of my sin so I'll carry the pain of my shame." But Jesus says, "I bore that too." And He beckons us to repentance and to receive mercy and forgiveness. But rather than repent we hold our sins out in our hands before Him and we say, "But this is what I've done." In response, Jesus holds His nail-pierced hands before us and says, "Yes. But this is what I've done."

You are forgiven. You are clean. You are free.

A very powerful passage I read when my heart needs to be reminded of the shame Jesus absorbed on my behalf is in Isaiah 53.

> Read Isaiah 53, really looking at verses 1-4 and 7-9. What resonates with you from these verses? What is most meaningful?

Jesus *willingly* absorbed our sin and shame on the cross and endured brutal separation from His Father so that we could live in freedom now. That wrecks me.

Shame is robbing us of living in the freedom and fullness of life that Christ purchased for us.

> How has shame robbed you? What lies have you believed?

Shame lies and tells us that because we do unlovable things, we are unlovable people. Shame says you are a mistake. It associates what we do, or what is done to us, with the very essence of who we are. It is very real, painful, and none of us are immune to it.

In fact, pastor and author Scott Sauls writes this about shame:

> The longer I am a pastor, the more convinced I become that every person, regardless of her or his situation, is fighting a hidden battle with shame. Shame, the greatest enemy of God's grace and also the greatest inhibitor of truth, justice, and human love, is something that must be addressed. ... The vague sense that there is something deeply wrong with us compels us to hide, blame, and run for cover. Left to ourselves, we are restlessly turned inward and desperately committed to some kind of self-salvation strategy. We work hard to create a counter-narrative to the shaming voice within and without. ... What if there were a way for the cycle of shame to be broken in our lives? ... My greatest joy as a Christian pastor is that I get to tell people that such a remedy exists. When Jesus allowed himself to be stripped naked, spit upon, taunted, rejected, and made nothing on the cross—when he, the one who had nothing to be ashamed of, surrendered to the ruthless, relentless shaming that led to our redemption and healing—he accomplished our liberation from shame.[5]

Jesus accomplishes your liberation from shame! Will you just sit with that for a moment and invite God to melt your heart with that good news?

Now I realize you may only be a casual acquaintance with shame or you may be shame's best friend. But one thing's for sure: if we've allowed shame to hang out in our hearts, it's likely we've parented with shame, because what we live in is what we live out.

Shame begets shame. But grace begets grace.

I hear from moms all of the time who are living in shame over their inability to be a "good enough" mom and are projecting shame onto their kids when they aren't measuring up to unrealistic expectations.

One mom recently wrote to me through my blog, "Thank you for writing so honestly about your parenting fails and God's forgiveness. It makes me feel not so alone in my own failure. My daughter had incredibly bad behavior this week. I get so angry and find it hard to forgive her for how she acts. Then I find it hard to forgive myself for my reaction to her. It's a vicious cycle. This parenting thing makes me feel so much shame but I don't know what else to do."

As that email demonstrates, we all have a merciless critic in our heads that speaks condemnation to our hearts. That's the bad news.

But here's the good news. We have a merciful Savior who hung on a cross, bearing the weight of our shame, so that we could walk in freedom from it.

Which voice do you tend to listen to?

CONDEMNATION --- CONVICTION

Condemnation comes from the enemy. It's the voice of shame, wanting us to believe our heavenly Father is shaking His head in disappointment and disgust with His arms crossed and His heart closed to us.

Conviction comes from the Holy Spirit. It's the voice of grace, beckoning us to run to Jesus, repent, receive mercy, and run the race before us in His transforming power and grace:

> For all have sinned and fall short of the glory of God. They are justified freely by his grace through the redemption that is in Christ Jesus.
> ROMANS 3:23-24

What we live in is what we live out.

Which voice are we going to listen to, my friends?

To put shame in its rightful place, we have to receive the mercy and grace of God and enjoy the identity given to us by God in Jesus Christ.

You are fully known.

You are fully accepted.

You are fully loved.

That is who you really are! And that is the essence of the gospel—the good news—that you and I need to be reminded of daily—perhaps hourly.

This is the truth of God's Word.

> *When we were utterly helpless, Christ came at just the right time and died for us sinners. Now, most people would not be willing to die for an upright person, though someone might perhaps be willing to die for a person who is especially good. But God showed his great love for us by sending Christ to die for us while we were still sinners.*
> ROMANS 5:6-8, NLT

Did you catch that? *"While we were still sinners."* At our worst and at our darkest Jesus gave His life for us. Jesus absorbed every ounce of sin and shame for you and for me on the cross. Jesus wants our sin to lead us to repentance and greater reliance on the Holy Spirit. When we live in the assurance that we have been forgiven of our sin, we are liberated from our shame. In that place we are freed to humbly testify to the grace of God with our children.

Are you so entangled in sin and held captive to shame that you cannot fathom a God who would welcome you right now, just as you are? I have good news for you. Jesus loves to forgive sinners. It is precisely you for whom Jesus came, and He's not going anywhere without you. He won't leave you where He found you.

CLOSE WITH PRAYER
Father, thank You that You fully see me and fully love me. Help me to release the shame I feel for the mistakes I have made and to live daily in the grace You have shown me through Your Son.

We've done the hard and holy work this week. Thank you for being brave. I know our Father is so delighted to see us grow in grace and receive His love!

We want our hearts to be strengthened by grace, because grace then becomes a fountain that flows from us. Grace in our hearts becomes grace in our words and actions.

We need to feed our hearts with gospel truths every day.

> Read Ephesians 3:14-21. How does it speak to this inner strengthening?

Let us never underestimate the power He has given us to overcome the sins and shortcomings that keep us from being the mothers we long to be for our kids. The same power that raised Christ Jesus from the dead is available to us in daily mothering.

> Think about this verse as we close today:

> *And God is able to make all grace abound to you, so that having all sufficiency in all things at all times, you may abound in every good work.*
> 2 CORINTHIANS 9:8, ESV

When you say goodnight to your children and Satan throws today's failures in your face, you feel overwhelmed by the mere prospect of tomorrow, and hope is in limited supply, remember God's amazing grace. By grace, we are saved, sanctified, and strengthened so that we might fulfill our significant calling as moms.

Grace in our hearts becomes grace in our words and actions.

In Jesus we are rescued from the penalty of our sin, we have ongoing forgiveness for our sin, and we have the promised help of Christ to help fight sin and grow in grace. We are clean; we are free!

CLOSE WITH PRAYER

Read the following verses, and then write your thoughts and prayers based on the Scripture.

> *For this reason I kneel before the Father from whom every family in heaven and on earth is named. I pray that he may grant you, according to the riches of his glory, to be strengthened with power in your inner being through his Spirit, and that Christ may dwell in your hearts through faith. I pray that you, being rooted and firmly established in love, may be able to comprehend with all the saints what is the length and width, height and depth of God's love, and to know Christ's love that surpasses knowledge, so that you may be filled with all the fullness of God. Now to him who is able to do above and beyond all that we ask or think according to the power that works in us—to him be glory in the church and in Christ Jesus to all generations, forever and ever. Amen.*
> **EPHESIANS 3:14-21**

For freedom, Christ set us free.

GALATIANS 5:1a

LIVING IN FREEDOM

Group Discussion Questions

1. What is the difference between condemnation and conviction?

2. Why is it so hard to be honest with ourselves and with God about our sin?

3. Read Galatians 5:1. What is the "yoke of slavery" you feel? What burdens you most, filling you with shame, guilt, and frustration?

4. How would believing that you are God's dearly loved daughter change the way you live each day? The way you respond to others? The way you respond to your children?

5. We are halfway through the study. What do you sense God most wants you to know? What continues to be your biggest challenge?

6. What changes have you made in your parenting as a result of meeting with this group and doing this Bible study?

_____

_____

_____

_____

_____

_____

_____

To hear more from Jeannie,
download the optional video
bundle at lifeway.com/momsetfree

We are going to begin this week exploring a word that probably holds different meanings for each of us: brokenness.

When you think of the word *brokenness*, what comes to mind?

I've tended to think of brokenness as merely a feeling that results from something bad I've done or something bad that has happened to me. But here's what I'm learning: Brokenness isn't just a feeling we have or a season we walk through. It is actually the state in which we exist and live.

If we're breathing, we're broken.

Because of the fall, we enter this world sinful, fallen, broken people. We are broken people living in a world that has been broken by sin. It is part of who we are and who we will be until we are with Jesus. As Brennan Manning said, "To be alive is to be broken. And to be broken is to stand in need of grace."[1]

So essentially, if we're breathing, we're broken. And if we're broken, we're in need of Christ. However, needing Christ is never, ever a bad thing. In fact, our desire should never be to need Jesus less. It should be to become more and more aware of our need for Him and to draw closer and closer to Him, where lasting hope is found and genuine transformation occurs.

So, the bad news of our brokenness is actually the doorway to the good news. Only when we accept how far we fall short of God's holy requirements can we begin to embrace and celebrate the necessity of God's grace.

Whole—or perfect—is the hope and promise of what we are ultimately going to be when He comes again.

Read 1 Corinthians 13:12. Write it below.

Because Jesus was broken for us, we will, for all eternity, be whole. So while we are already perfect in Christ, we are not yet whole in the flesh. We are no longer who we once were—dead because of our sin. We have been made alive in Christ and given a place with Him in eternity, but we are not yet fully transformed. We are becoming (Eph. 2:1-7).

So I just want to encourage you. If you don't feel whole, or if you don't feel like God has glued all your pieces back together so that no cracks remain, don't lose hope. It doesn't mean God's not at work in your life. He is indeed at work, wooing you to Himself and crafting you in His likeness. He will make good on His promise of wholeness when sin is wiped out for good. In the meantime, His love and light inside you can shine through your cracks, to the glory of His grace.

So what shall we do with our brokenness until then? We bring our brokenness to God, because, if we look to Scripture, what we find is that His specialty is rescuing and redeeming broken people and carrying out His purpose through them.

Read Luke 22:54-62. How many times did Peter deny knowing Jesus?

If there was ever someone whom we'd expect Jesus to say, "You've messed up too big and your sin is too great and your value is now void," it's Peter.

Read John 21:15-19. What did Jesus ask Peter?

How many times did Jesus ask?

What did Jesus tell Peter to do after each answer?

Jesus welcomed Peter just after the depths of his brokenness and sinfulness were revealed. Jesus invited Peter to confirm His love for Him, and He commissioned him. Peter repented. Jesus restored. And Jesus did so knowing Peter would fail Him again. That he would fail to walk in step with *"the truth of the gospel"* (GAL. 2:14).

Notice how Jesus didn't ask, "Can I trust you not to fail Me again?"

What did He ask instead?

Jesus wants our love. We've unearthed this truth already. He knows that if He has our love, obedience and good works will follow.

We are prone to believe that God is counting on us to get it all right, and when we get it all wrong, one of the things we do best is "promise we will do better tomorrow." I can't tell you the number of nights I put the kids to bed after a terribly defeating day when the depths of my humanity and sinfulness were revealed through my parenting and so I promised God "I'll do better tomorrow."

We forget that Jesus doesn't forgive and restore based on our promise to do better tomorrow, as demonstrated through Peter. He restores us out of His extravagant grace. We also forget that Jesus wants our hearts before He wants our effort, because He knows a heart surrendered to Him will produce fruit that our own effort and striving could never manufacture.

The *ESV Gospel Transformation Bible* on this passage says,

> God uses these real-life, flawed people as pictures of his loving and merciful kindness toward us. God cares most about our hearts, and even when we fail out of fear and rebellion he restores us out of his abundant grace. Such stories reveal God's heart of acceptance and forgiveness. When we understand God properly in this way, it creates in us a freedom to be honest and open about our weaknesses and failures, which is precisely the humility needed to approach God. Our acceptance of God's acceptance of us—free from condemnation, because of Christ (Rom. 8:1)—woos and draws us near to God and frees us from shame and fear.[2]

This grace should bring us extraordinary comfort.

- Grace beckons us to stop fighting our brokenness and embrace our belovedness.

- Grace allows us to be honest with ourselves about ourselves.

- Grace allows us to be honest with God about ourselves.

- Grace allows us to be honest with one another about ourselves.

- Grace allows us to be honest with our children about ourselves.

Which of these statements about grace means the most to you right now?

Grace beckons us to stop fighting our brokenness and embrace our belovedness.

It's OK to admit you're not OK. We can be honest about it because we have a Savior who was more than OK. He was perfect. And He has us covered. Oh, sweet freedom!

But if we don't live by grace we will see a very different story unfold. We will live in shame, perpetually trying to prove that we are good-enough. Exhausted and worn out. Never living in the fullness of His love. And incapable of leading our kids in the freedom they crave.

CLOSE WITH PRAYER

Lord, please help me to see myself as Your beloved. Allow Your grace to replace all the insecurities, fears, and mistakes that keep me from finding freedom in You. Allow me to rest in knowing You are enough so that I don't have to be.

Today, we are going to explore the Sermon on the Mount in Matthew 5–7. You should know, these three chapters used to make me feel so much pressure and create so much angst in my pursuit of perfection. So I'm excited to explore this passage with you and see how it actually points us to our freedom in Christ.

In Matthew 5–7, we find the Sermon on the Mount. Jesus *"saw the crowds, he went up on the mountain, and after he sat down, his disciples came to him. Then he began to teach them"* **(MATT. 5:1-2).** Jesus taught His disciples about happiness, worry, the kingdom of heaven, adultery, and more.

Write Matthew 5:48.

What feelings or reaction does this verse evoke for you?

Do you think it is possible to follow its command? Why or why not?

I have had conversations with enough women to know I'm not the only one who has felt the pressure to be perfect in order to keep God's pleasure and worried that God was angry with me because I couldn't live up to this impossible standard. While we know deep down we cannot be perfect, we try. Oh, how we try.

Skim through the rest of Matthew 5–7. What common themes do you see emerging?

In the Sermon on the Mount, Jesus shows us that no matter how hard we try, we cannot be good enough on our own. We can't be perfect. We can't live up to the standards He sets in these chapters.

This seems like bad news, right? It is actually the way to freedom. Hang with me, friend. In the Sermon on the Mount, like with the Law of Moses, God reveals our brokenness and desperation so that we will be set free from trying to be impossibly righteous. Knowing we cannot do it on our own, we will fall in awe and wonder at the One who achieved righteousness for us.

Read and reflect on Romans 3:20-24. According to these verses, how are we made righteous?

What do these verses tell us about the way God looks at our brokenness?

When we believe in Christ and trust Him as our Savior, we take on His righteousness. God sees the beauty and goodness of His Son covering you and me.

Knowing we are loved by God and covered in the righteousness of Christ, just as we are, ignites a love for Jesus and inspires a desire to fulfill the commandment on which all others are built:

For this is what love for God is: to keep his commands. And his commands are not a burden.
1 JOHN 5:3

God sees the beauty and goodness of His Son covering you and me.

Grace stimulates gratitude, and gratitude inspires obedience.

We will desire to glorify God in humble response to the grace He has shown us in Jesus. Grace stimulates gratitude, and gratitude inspires obedience.

Obedience is the manifestation of a heart that knows it is saved by grace alone and loved without limits.

Accepting that we are accepted in Christ creates a new dynamic for obedience. The radical love of Jesus is not only freeing, it's transformational. Knowing the lengths to which Jesus went to rescue us opens us up to the Holy Spirit's transforming work in our lives.

Thus, sin, or disobedience, is ingratitude for what God did for us in the humiliation and exhalation of Jesus Christ. While it may sting to think of our sin that way, we must. We cannot minimize it. Disobedience isn't just breaking the rules; it's the rejection of the richness of God's grace in Jesus Christ.

Our sin can and does have devastating consequences on our lives and the lives of our children. We cannot take sin lightly, just as God does not take sin lightly, because sin *"gives birth to death"* **(JAS. 1:15).** My sin is what nailed my Savior to the cross. There is nothing about that to be celebrated. What is worthy of celebration is that my sinless Savior conquered my sin-stained life on the cross, securing my acceptance before God.

It's only when we are willing to take a good, long look at the gravity and magnitude of our sin that God's grace leads us to repentance from our sin and a desire to turn toward relying on His Spirit to grow us in righteousness. Rather than strive for perfection, we should seek to grow in grace. Growing in grace promotes other godly works in us.

As Paul says, grace in our lives is *"not in vain"* **(1 COR. 15:10).**

Read 1 Corinthians 15:9-10, and fill in the chart below with which sections of the verses point to the traits in the right column. I've done the first one for you.

"I am the least of the apostles, not worthy to be called an apostle."	Humility
	Authenticity
	Gratitude
	A new identity
	Desire
	Glory to the Giver of grace

CLOSE WITH PRAYER

Father, thank You for Your perfect Son making a way for me to be perfect. Forgive me for my sins. Help me to celebrate the grace You've given and grow in grace into Your likeness. Amen.

Let's turn right to God's Word, and read two sentences that hold the good news for moms who are tired of trying to be good enough.

> *For freedom, Christ set us free. Stand firm then and don't submit again*
> *to a yoke of slavery.*
> GALATIANS 5:1

We've been set free for what?

We were set free to be free. That is who we are as believers—free from sin and death. Free to walk in Christ and live in the abundance of Him.

What is the "yoke of slavery" Paul was referring to in Galatians 5:1?

As one commentary puts it, the yoke of slavery is "the burden of the rigorous demands of the law as the means for gaining God's favor—an intolerable burden for sinful humanity."[4]

The yoke of slavery is the oppression of trying to be enough on our own. But through Jesus, God tells us the intolerable burden of trying to keep God pleased and happy is lifted.

Some see freedom as the ability to do whatever we want, to live however we please. Our culture tells us we can find happiness and fulfillment in that. Sometimes we look at the verses on grace and think that's what God is telling us, too. But if we've spent any time seeking this sort of freedom, a selfish freedom, we know it's a freedom full of empty promises. This phony freedom always leads to disappointment and destruction.

Phony freedom is rooted in our performance—how good we've been or how hard we've been trying to be a *good Christian*. But that, my friend, is not freedom. That is slavery.

When we live in phony freedom, we are living oppressed. We are living enslaved to the pressure to be perfect, to be enough, to be righteous all on our own. We cannot maintain that lifestyle. That is not why Christ set us free.

When have you lived in a phony freedom?

What were the results of living in that phony freedom?

Christ set us free to be free. He set us free from striving to be enough. The cross of Christ, not our performance or progress, makes us pleasing to God. Allowing this truth to melt our hearts does not make us want to indulge our sinful nature. It makes us desire to stay close to Him, do life like Him, and love others like He does. In other words, "Because of who God is and what he has done for believers in Jesus Christ, Christians are commanded to 'become what they are,' that is, to make visible in the earthly realm of their human existence what God has already declared and sealed in the divine verdict of justification."[3]

Read Romans 6:11-14. What does verse 14 say we are under now?

What does it mean for you personally to live under grace rather than under the law?

How does living under grace change your daily interaction with your children?

Freedom comes only through being found in Christ. In knowing that you are completely, head-to-toe, inside and out, covered in the perfection of Christ. Freedom is believing that every square inch of you is worthy of love and belonging simply because you are His.

There are essentially three ways to go about life:

1. We can live ignoring or rejecting God's love and acceptance all together.

2. We can live for God's love and acceptance.

3. We can live from God's love and acceptance.

Which way do you tend to go about life?

How does that approach to life impact your parenting?

Let's look more closely at these three different approaches.

1. LIVING BY IGNORING OR REJECTING GOD'S LOVE AND ACCEPTANCE ALL TOGETHER

To ignore or reject God's love is simply the way of self-approval. This stems from our culture's insistence that we just need to do a better job loving ourselves because we're really not that bad. What we don't realize is that even this way of living is a form of slavery—we are enslaved to ourselves. We try to minimize the magnitude of our sins and shortcomings so we can feel better about how we're doing, when in truth, what we really need is to be rescued from ourselves.

This is not to suggest that we should see ourselves as worthless. Luke 12:7 makes it clear to us that we are of great worth in God's eyes. However, nowhere in Scripture do we find God telling us to do a better job of loving ourselves. Rather, He tells us to do what?

Read Matthew 22:37-40. What are the two commandments in this passage?

Read 1 John 4:16.

We are to know and believe in God's love for us. His is the only steadfast, unwavering love.

2. LIVING FOR GOD'S LOVE AND ACCEPTANCE

When we are living for God's love and acceptance, we are trying to earn and keep His pleasure. We are constantly striving to do better and try harder. We're trying to be good Christians in order to make God happy.

I've tried that approach. Maybe you have, too. If so, you have probably seen, like I have, that no matter how hard we try, it is impossible to keep going at that pace. As we're striving to be enough, we keep bumping into our brokenness, stumbling over our sin, and feeling weighed down by our weaknesses. We will eventually collapse, if not literally out of exhaustion, then metaphorically from soul dehydration.

How have you seen yourself trying to live for God's love?

What were the results of living this way?

How do you see this manifesting itself in your parenting? Do you see your kids living for God's love or for your love?

If so, what are some practical steps you can take to begin to steer them in a different direction?

We're not alone in trying to live for God's love. The apostle Paul tried it too.

READ GALATIANS 2:15-16 FROM THE MESSAGE:

We Jews know that we have no advantage of birth over "non-Jewish sinners." We know very well that we are not set right with God by rule-keeping but only through personal faith in Jesus Christ. How do we know? We tried it—and we had the best system of rules the world has ever seen! Convinced that no human being can please God by self-improvement, we believed in Jesus as the Messiah so that we might be set right before God by trusting in the Messiah, not by trying to be good.

3. LIVING FROM GOD'S LOVE AND ACCEPTANCE

Living from God's love leads to freedom from striving for what is already ours in Christ. We are free from slavery to self-reliance, free from proving we are worthy of love and belonging. Free to shed our shame and embrace our true identities in Christ as God's beloved.

Read 1 John 3:1. According to this verse, who are we?

Read Titus 3:4-7. Put these verses in your own words, writing them as a prayer of thanksgiving.

When we live from God's love we find that our "delight is in the LORD's instruction, and [we meditate] on it day and night" (Ps. 1:2). And we finally discover the true rest our souls crave. The kind that empowers us in our parenting.

This may seem a little silly, but friend, I want you to pause here and say this out loud:

"I am the one Jesus loves."

The song we sing with our kids over and over and over still holds true for us: "Jesus loves me, this I know."

In light of what we've read today, what emotions do those statements evoke in you?

When we live believing we are loved by Christ, we will begin to thrive instead of strive. We will live set free. We are set free not to earn, perform, strive, prove, sin, or try harder. We are set free to love.

Read Galatians 5:13. What are we to use our freedom to do?

What steps can you take today to begin living as one loved by God?

How would living this way change the way you parent?

How can you serve your children through love as an outpouring of living set free?

We are set free to love.

CLOSE WITH PRAYER

If there is any iota of you that is still trying to earn God's affection and pleasure through your own goodness, and you have yet to feel the grace of God deep in your bones, I'd like to invite you to pause and personalize what you've read today. In fact, this invitation isn't just for those who are still trying to earn God's pleasure. It's for all of us. We need to be reminded over and over again of the freedom for which Christ has set us free. So no matter where you are on the spectrum, will you join me in praising God for being set free?

Lord, You have set me free. You have called me by name and I belong to You. I am of great worth in Your eyes, Lord. I don't have to fear Your rejection. I do not have to be afraid of losing Your affection. You have saved me from proving I am worthy. You love me and You will never, ever forsake me. Lord, help me believe what You've promised to me and what You say about me is true. Help me live like it's true, because it is.

DAY 4

My family is a very expressive family. We love to demonstrate our love. In words, in sticky notes, in physical affection, in interpretive dance. OK, maybe not through interpretive dance. Actually, yes, through interpretive dance. Goofy is my thing. I digress.

When we say to our two older boys, "I love you," they respond as you'd expect. They smile and sweetly say "I love you, too." But, when we tell Owen, our third son, that we love him, he's always had a unique response. He will very tenderly smile and respond, "I know," before he says, "I love you, too."

When Owen says those two simple words—"I know"—he blesses me with his confidence in my love. It melts my heart to know he knows how very much he is loved by me. And it makes me think perhaps we bless Jesus with our confidence in His love for us.

As a parent, I don't want my children to think they have to work to earn my love and approval. That would break my heart. I would do anything to assure them there was nothing they could do to make me love them more or make me love them less. I love them just because I love them. That will never change. I'm sure you're nodding your head in agreement about your children.

As I've said before, I used to think Jesus was pleased to see me working hard to earn His approval and love. It didn't occur to me that my repentance and my rest in His saving work and unconditional love brought Him pleasure.

Have you ever felt that way? Explain.

Friend, our heavenly Father longs for us to accept our acceptance in Christ. And the path to receiving His acceptance is through repentance.

This is what the Sovereign LORD, the Holy One of Israel, says:

"In repentance and rest is your salvation,
in quietness and trust is your strength,
but you would have none of it."
ISAIAH 30:15, NIV

Oh, how those seven words pierce me: "But you would have none of it." How often that is me.

Have you been there? What has God asked of you that you would have none of?

In times like that, I need to remember the gospel I have forgotten. Martin Luther is credited for saying, "We need to hear the gospel every day because we forget it every day."

Explain the gospel (the good news of Jesus) as you understand it.

How can you incorporate hearing the gospel message into your everyday life more?

For me, it comes down to rest. When I am pursuing self-perfection, when I am trying to earn God's love, I am restless. But when I anchor my identity in Christ and His perfection, rest enfolds my heart. We've been personally invited to trade our trying and shame for repentance and rest. When we rest in what God has done through His Son, we can be set free.

How do we set our hearts at rest when our hearts condemn us? First, we need to believe what God says in His Word.

Read 1 John 3:19-24. What does this passage say about our hearts?

How well does God know us?

God knows *everything*. Nothing is hidden from Him, and everything can be forgiven by Him. He knows us better than we know ourselves. Because He has forgiven us, we no longer have to be weighed down by our failures. We are free to rest in the righteousness of Christ.

I love how Paul says it in Galatians 2:19-21. Read those verses.

This is as close to a checklist for "How to Live in the Freedom and Fullness of God's Love" as we're going to get.

Read each item below taken from The Message paraphrase of those verses and record one way you can begin to implement each item into your daily life:

Quit trying to please God by keeping the rules.

Identify yourself completely with Christ.

Stop trying to impress God.

Live by faith in Christ's work on your behalf.

Refuse to reject God's grace.

It's not your typical checklist. Instead of a to-do list, it's almost a quit-doing list. But that's how it is with grace.

> Which task on the checklist would be easiest for you?

> Which would be the most difficult?

> How would your parenting look different if you implemented the checklist?

We are free to rest in the righteousness of Christ.

CLOSE WITH PRAYER

Lord Jesus, thank You for the good news, for Your story, the gospel. Thank You for the hope it brings. Help me to rest in You. Amen.

DAY 5

Take some time to answer these questions as you spend time with the Lord.

Do you feel like you often settle for less-than when it comes to life with Christ? How so?

Why do we so often settle for just a little of Jesus when He wants to give us all of Him?

There is no part of His power, His grace, His forgiveness, His mercy, or His joy that is off limits to us.

What kind of freedom would you be walking in if you really believed that God can't stop loving you?

What burdens would be laid down? What shame would you shed? What striving would you cease?

He is so rich in kindness and grace that he purchased our freedom with the blood of his Son and forgave our sins.
EPHESIANS 1:7, NLT

My friend, the price was paid and the point was made. You are free! Are you ready to parent like that's true?

CLOSE WITH PRAYER
Write a prayer asking God for His grace and mercy over your life. Thank Him for paying the price for your freedom. Praise Him for His faithfulness. Commit to trust Jesus with everything, including your kids.

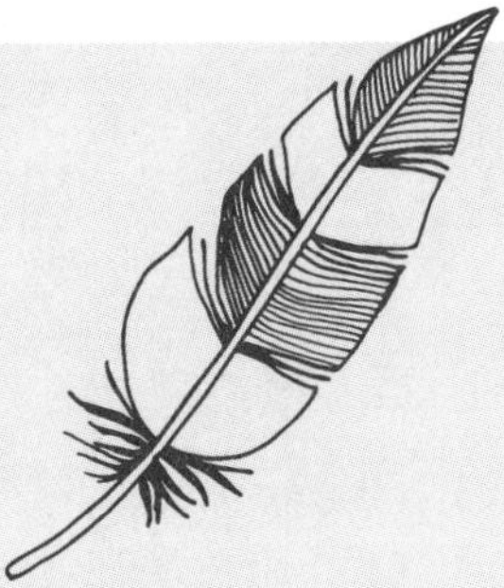

_____

_____

_____

_____

_____

_____

_____

_____

_____

_____

_____

_____

_____

_____

_____

_____

_____

_____

_____

_____

_____

_____

_____

_____

_____

Grace opens hearts to repentance and transformation.

#MOMSETFREE

FREEDOM IN TRANSFORMATION

Group Discussion Questions

1. What parenting burdens have you laid down and entrusted to God in the previous weeks?

2. How have you learned to receive God's grace?

3. Read 1 Corinthians 13:4-7. Only God's love is pure and perfect, but what are some tangible ways that we can demonstrate God's love to our children?

4. Read 1 John 3:1. How can we anchor our children and their identity in God's lavish love?

5. As you spend more time in God's Word and among His people, how is He transforming your mind and heart?

6. What are the benefits of living in the freedom and fullness of God's love?

7. How are these changes and benefits spilling over to your children?

_____

_____

_____

_____

_____

_____

To hear more from Jeannie,
download the optional video
bundle at lifeway.com/momsetfree

DAY 1

We have come so far in our four weeks together, haven't we? We have pushed back the pressure with the promises of God and laid down what God has not asked us to carry as moms. We have discovered how the good news frees us from the pressure to pretend we have it all together for one another and the pressure to perform for the acceptance of God.

Shame and striving have been exchanged for repentance and rest.

And now we are ready—more than ready—to see how accepting God's grace for us empowers us to parent our children with the unconditional love that God has first given us in Christ.

I'm praying that after what we've journeyed through together, we will undoubtedly witness the good news in our hearts overflowing into our homes. In our motives, in our desires, in our attitudes, in our words, and in our actions, I am praying we will see the gospel manifest itself in our parenting.

But, again, this isn't an invitation to sit back and assume there is nothing for us to do except revel in grace. God wants us to take what we've discovered and make every effort, by the power of the Holy Spirit, to now:

- establish a gospel-centered pattern of parenting;

- implement practices that will make grace reverberate throughout our homes;

- lead our kids in living in the freedom of Christ; and

- then trust Him with the children He's entrusted to us.

Yes! I think this is what we've been waiting for. It's time to take what we've learned about how to live as moms set free and apply it to our parenting—to help our kids live in the freedom for which Christ has set them free. Or better said, in the words of my pal Elisabeth, to help them live as kids set free.

So we are circling back to how we concluded Week 2 of our study. We read in Deuteronomy 6 and in Matthew 22 that our primary purpose is to raise children who love the Lord with all their hearts, souls, and minds. And we discovered that

the way in which Scripture guides us in doing that is actually quite simple, right? (We're not confusing simple with easy.) We raise children who love God by teaching them how much God, in Jesus Christ, loved them first (1 John 4:19). In other words, we make the good news everything. Because it is everything.

Now, I love research. It's fair to call me a research junkie. And so I can't help but share with you just one piece of research I recently stumbled upon that actually confirms the essentialness of a gospel-centered framework (not to be confused with "formula") for parenting. The enemy is going to ruthlessly and persistently tempt us to believe the gospel should be peripheral at best, and is superfluous at worst, in our parenting. But nothing could be further from the truth.

I'm sure we are all aware of the research about how younger generations are leaving the church in droves. But what about the kids who aren't leaving? What about the kids who are staying and serving and growing deeper in their faith? What made the difference?

The research revealed that the common thread found in twenty-somethings who were living out their faith was simply this: growing up in a home where the parents "... ultimately operated from a framework of grace that held up the cross of Jesus as the basis for peace with God and forgiveness toward one another."[1]

Not parents who operated from a framework of rigid rules. Not parents who held up their own perfection as the basis for peace with God. But parents who operated from a framework of grace, my friends. That is our goal for the next two weeks—to discover how to parent from a framework of grace. And you know what? Christ has given us everything we need to do just that. We have the power of God's Spirit, God's Word, and God's grace in our own hearts, ready to be poured into our homes and our children's hearts.

Shame and striving have been exchanged for repentance and rest.

Would you say you currently parent from a framework of grace? If so, how did you get there? If not, what would need to change to get you there?

Will you remember with me what we learned about how our own journey to living in freedom begins? It requires:

- acknowledging who we are apart from Christ; and

- anchoring our identities in who we are in Christ.

Well, it's no different with our children. That being said, I'd be lying if I didn't tell you there was a time when I was hesitant to talk to my kids about who they are apart from Christ. Oh, I couldn't wait to feed their hearts with the truths about who they are in Christ. I just feared telling them the truth about their sinful, fallen nature.

Why do you think it's challenging to talk about our fallen, sinful nature?

But here's the thing. Even if we aren't talking with our children about their sinful and broken nature, they know it exists. And just like us, they feel the burden of it. They can try to squash it or deny it or talk self-love to it, and that might even work ... for a bit.

Read 1 John 1:8-10. If we claim we are free of sin, what two things does this passage say we do to ourselves?

And what do we do to God?

There is only one cure to the crushing reality of our sinful nature, and His beautiful name is Jesus. It isn't until we get honest about who we are without Him that we can become grateful for who we are *in Him*.

> Read 2 Corinthians 5:17. When we are in Christ, what do we become?

We remain sinful in the flesh, and yet, at the very same time, our identity is 100 percent righteous to the core before God when we are in Christ. And all because of Jesus, we are "a new creation."

If we want to make the gospel central in our homes and operate from a framework of grace, two things need to happen:

- We have to give our children the bad news so they can see themselves for who they really are—in the flesh—before their holy God.

- We have to give our children the good news so they can see Jesus for who He truly is and who they are in Him.

In the chart below, use the verses listed to fill in some of the characteristics of who we are in Christ. I've done the first one for you.

WHO WE ARE IN THE FLESH	WHO WE ARE IN CHRIST
Sinful	Hebrews 10:10—Sanctified (made fit for God's holy purpose)
Fallen	Ephesians 1:7—
Rebellious	2 Corinthians 5:21—
Broken	1 John 3:2—

These two things go hand in hand. If we only talk about our children's sinful nature, we will leave them drowning in despair, and the song that will likely play on repeat in their heads is, "I am bad. I am bad. I will always be bad."

But if we talk only about how loved they are by God, we will lead them down the path of pride and ingratitude for Jesus. The song that will likely play on repeat in their heads will sound more like, "I am good. All is love. I don't need a Savior."

God's love for our kids, and God's forgiveness of our kids, is secure *because* of the person and work of Jesus Christ (see Isa. 53:5-6).

Helping our children see the reality of their sinful nature is what will inspire them to fall in love with the One who takes great pleasure in transforming broken sinners into beloved children of God. They are free to confess how desperately sinful they are and free to celebrate how deeply loved they are in Christ. The bad news of our sinful nature always leads us to the good news of our sinless Savior who loved us and gave Himself for us.

Read Romans 6:1-14. What have we been set free from, according to verse 7?

Verse 14 in the NLT reads, *"Sin is no longer your master, for you no longer live under the requirements of the law. Instead, you live under the freedom of God's grace."*

The message for our children is this: *You have been set free from the power of sin. Be who you are in Christ by the power of the Holy Spirit.* The resurrection of Jesus Christ empowers change in our children's lives. Today. The same power that raised Jesus Christ from the dead is for them too, and it's for now.

Read Colossians 3:1-11. How do we become like Christ?

When our children sin, we can remind them: *Remember who you are in Christ. That behavior is your old sinful nature. You are a new creation in Christ. Ask Jesus to help you be who He made you to be. Through the resurrection power of Christ, fight against your sin by determining to be who you already are in Jesus.*

If your children do not believe yet, you can use moments of sin and disobedience to remind them this is why we all need Jesus. We need the Holy Spirit to work in our lives. We need a rescuer, a helper, to help us be who God created us to be.

Journal here how you might put this truth in your own words to your children.

We need the Holy Spirit to work in our lives.

While this language may seem foreign to you or impossible to incorporate into how you currently talk with your kids, it is indeed doable and can even become natural as you begin to make it part of your daily dialogue with your children. The more we feed our own hearts with these truths, the more naturally they will overflow into our parenting.

This is the message of extravagant grace and the sure foundation on which we can build.

Now, let's be reminded of our significance in light of God's sovereignty. No matter how hard we try, we don't hold the power to control what our children's hearts believe. We can no more make them see their need for a Savior than we can convince them how deeply loved they are by God. We can't make them accept their acceptance in Christ or see themselves through God's lens of grace. Only the Holy Spirit can do that. What we can do, however—what we have been called by God to do—is feed their hearts with the good news and pray that the Holy Spirit will enlighten their hearts to believe it.

CLOSE WITH PRAYER

Father, help my children see themselves through Your lens of grace. Give them hearts exploding with gratitude for the gift of Your Son, Jesus Christ, who rescued us by grace and makes us fit for Your holy purpose by grace. God, help our children rely on Your power inside them to be who You created them to be. Help them remember that they can't be who they long to be without You. It's simply impossible to live in the likeness of Christ without the power of Christ.

Before God led me down the path of writing and speaking, I was an adoption social worker. It was my dream job. Something I knew I wanted to do from my youth. I had the privilege of counseling women who were walking through unplanned pregnancies. I had the thrill of traveling the country, training health care counselors how to present adoption as a positive option to their clients. I had the joy of recruiting families for children in our foster care system. And finally, I had the honor of helping prospective adoptive couples welcome a child into their family.

Our kids are asking, "Is who I am enough?"

Part of my job, in this last role, was to conduct a series of interviews with each prospective adoptive couple to assess their readiness to adopt, to educate them about the process, and to provide parenting education.

During the interviews, one of the most important questions I was required to ask prospective parents is this:

Please tell me about your own parents. What would you emulate, and what would you change?

Each prospective adoptive parent brought a unique story to the table, but there was typically a common theme woven into their reflection about what they'd want to change in their own parenting. I think you'll quickly notice that theme in their comments below.

"I had good parents but ... I never felt like I lived up to my dad's expectations."

"I had good parents but ... I felt a lot of pressure to be a perfect child."

"I had good parents but ... I often felt like I couldn't do enough to keep them pleased."

The "but" almost always has to do with feeling like they were not enough. This was usually the one thing prospective adoptive parents wanted to be sure they did differently. And for those who didn't feel the pressure to prove they were enough, it was the one thing they typically wanted to emulate with their own kids.

How would you answer that question about your parents? What would you emulate? What would you change?

This is a really important discussion because our kids aren't just looking for the answer to the question we explored yesterday, *Who am I?* They also want to know, *Is who I am enough?*

See, we parents aren't the only ones linking accomplishment to acceptance and success to significance. Our kids are attempting to answer the question, *Is who I am enough?,* by:

- how well they perform on the field;

- how much they excel in school;

- how many likes they get on their Instagram feed;

- how well they behave for us; and

- how well they follow the commandments in the Bible.

What other things would you add to this list?

How have you witnessed this pressure affect your child's life?

The primary message our children receive is that they'd better be the best at everything, and this leaves them afraid to reveal their inadequacies and insecurities, hiding behind the best version of themselves.

A friend recently shared this story with me, and with her permission I want to share it with you.

My daughter, who was in the fourth grade at the time, was overcome with anxiety. Almost paralyzing anxiety. It broke my heart as her mama to see her suffer, and to feel so powerless to help her. But, over time, she finally confessed that she felt like she had to be the perfect good little girl. And God opened my eyes to the painful truth that my daughter was living out my own issues with perfectionism. I had been encouraging this performance-based mentality in her with my own subtle comments and unrealistic expectations. My daughter's anxiety was God's invitation to me to find my worth in His grace, not in my works. I knew this was the only way I'd be able to raise my daughter to do the same.

How have you possibly passed the pressure you feel to prove you are enough onto your children?

What might God be inviting you to believe about His grace for you, so that you can be a vessel of that grace to your children?

I can wholeheartedly resonate with my friend's experience.

As you now know, I too was a woman who chased hard after perfection and witnessed the negative implications of that chase impact my kids. I was building my self-worth on my own goodness and my ability to keep God pleased with my good works. And because of that, and without even realizing it, I was teaching my children to do the same—to base their self-worth on their own goodness.

But the good news of the gospel is this: Our inherent worth was secured on the cross, and we now live covered by the perfect goodness of Christ on our behalf. Our kids don't need more self-worth. They need more Christ-worth.

For our children to live in the freedom and the fullness of the cross, we want our children's deepest awareness of themselves to be in their Christ-worth.

Read each way we find our worth in Christ and the correlating Scripture. Then record your thoughts.

1. He made me. He sees me. He knows me. All of me.

Psalm 139

Matthew 10:30

Acts 15:8

2. He welcomes me. He accepts me. He wants me. As I am.

John 6:37

Romans 15:7

Colossians 1:21-22

3. He loves me. He forgives me. He makes me more like Him by His grace.

Jeremiah 31:3

Lamentations 3:22-23

Ephesians 3:17-19

This is a confidence that can withstand any shame attack the enemy launches at our children's hearts.

I just know we have this in common. We want our kids to feel what we ourselves long to feel: safe. Safe to take off their masks and let down their guards. Safe to be honest about how fragile they feel.

He calls me beloved.

We want them to know that God's love for them, His pleasure in them, His delight over them, and His kindness toward them is wholly dependent on Christ's perfection, not their performance.

This is how we raise kids set free. So when the internal and external voices whisper lies to our children like, *You're unworthy of love and belonging. You're not measuring up. You're a disappointment,* they can fight back with the truth: *The only One who gets to define me is the One who created me and redeemed me; and He calls me beloved.*

READ JOHN 10:7-11:
Jesus said again, "Truly I tell you, I am the gate for the sheep. All who came before me are thieves and robbers, but the sheep didn't listen to them. I am the gate. If anyone enters by me, he will be saved and will come in and go out and find pasture. A thief comes only to steal and kill and destroy. I have come so that they may have life and have it in abundance. I am the good shepherd. The good shepherd lays down his life for the sheep."

Jesus assured us we have a very real enemy who does what?

What did Jesus come to give us?

Who does Jesus say He is?

What does the Good Shepherd do?

CLOSE WITH PRAYER

Father, thank You that Jesus is the Good Shepherd who knows each one of His flock by name. Thank You that Jesus has personally chosen to lay down His life for each one of us as if we were the only one. Thank You that I don't have to keep striving to be enough and that You desire to see me live the abundantly free life He died to give me.

DAY 3

Why can we parents be so tough on our kids? It's a question I have to ask myself more often than I'd like to admit.

Maybe it's because we are so tough on ourselves? We are over-burdened and burned out because we expect far too much from ourselves and, therefore, far too much from our kids. We pour out and pour out, but we rarely fill up. Self-care is shelved, and we run on empty tanks. We forget we aren't God. We forget grace.

Or maybe it's because we are going through something tough ourselves—something that has caused sadness or anger or disappointment to take up residence in our hearts, and it overflows onto the ones we love most.

A phone call with a friend recently confirmed how predictable this is. She said,

> My daughter has been a stressed out tyrant for the last three days. I couldn't figure out why she was so irritable and angry and distant. She's not even a full-blown teenager yet! I tried everything I know to make it stop, to no avail. But today it hit me. When I looked in the mirror I realized I was a stressed out tyrant. I was trying too hard to be strong and keep it all together while going through some really hard stuff at work and in my marriage. I didn't want my kids to see me as weak and unable. And because I was trying to pretend like I could handle it all, I took my stress out on my kids.

Maybe you can relate? I certainly can, which is why I'm so excited about what God wants to show us today and tomorrow.

Thankfully, we've already laid the foundation for this conversation. Back in Week 1, Day 4, we studied 2 Corinthians 12:7-10, and discovered what God's Word says about His grace being made perfect in our weakness. (If you need to take a moment to look back, please do. It's on page 27.)

Remember? We don't have to be ashamed of our weaknesses and need because Jesus loves to meet us, strengthen us, and glorify Himself through us in that place, by His grace. We are free to be honest about our weaknesses with our kids. Whew that's good news.

But now I want to ask you another question.

How free do you feel to be honest with your kids about your sin?

We must learn to walk alongside our children in brokenness.

Friend, that is where we are headed now, because, ultimately, we are free to be honest about both our weakness and our sin, because God's grace is sufficient for both.

Are you familiar with the stunning song, "Broken Together" by Casting Crowns? I can only imagine the number of marriages that have been healed and restored by God through the lyrics. They sing about how we won't be whole or complete, but that we can be "broken together."

This song encourages us to hold onto hope as we remember one another's humanity, walk alongside one another in humility, and fight for healing. What I love about this song is that it isn't just for marriage. It's for life. It's for our friendships. It's for our workplaces. And yes, it's even for our parenting. We must learn how to walk alongside our children in brokenness—to be broken together.

And yet, I know this is a very real challenge for a lot of us. Oh, I get it. For many years I tried desperately to hide my sinfulness from my kids. So whether you are the momma of a two year old or a thirty-two year old, I'm going to guess that you, too, don't love the idea of your children being privy to your humanity. We question, *How will they respect us and look up to us and obey us if they see us struggle?*

What else keeps you from confessing your sin to your children?

The unchangeable reality is that we (our children and us) are all sinners saved by grace. We are all broken. We all need Jesus.

Now this isn't at all to suggest that we want to submit to or celebrate our sin. God calls us to fight for victory over sin with His resurrection power that has been given to us as new creations in Christ.

Each one of these passages holds instruction on what to do with sin. After you look up each verse, note what we are called to do.

Romans 6:12

Ephesians 4:21-22

Colossians 3:5-6

Hebrews 3:12-13

What are followers of Jesus called to pursue?

Parenting with a "broken together" mind-set doesn't mean we give up our fight against sin and the devastating effects it has on our lives. And it doesn't mean we stop modeling a heart in pursuit of holiness. It's just the opposite, actually.

It means we create a culture of confession, not perfection, in our homes.

If we want to raise kids who tell the truth willingly and repent sincerely, we have to go first. When we are honest about our brokenness, we free our children to be honest about their brokenness. And grace is unleashed to do its transforming work in their hearts.

How do we create a culture of confession, not perfection? Well, when we get it wrong, we have to be willing to say the nine hardest words—"I am sorry. I was wrong. Please forgive me." We have to let our children see our willingness to confess our sinfulness because we know we have a Savior who willingly laid down His life to cover us.

Read the following verses and write down what they encourage us to do.

Matthew 5:23-34

James 5:16

Our children are not the exception to these verses, so we should stop allowing ourselves to believe they are.

Does the atmosphere in your home look more like confession or perfection? How does remembering your freedom in Christ allow you to create a home of confession?

Another benefit to remembering our own brokenness is that it makes us more compassionate—and less critical—toward the brokenness of our kids. When they get it wrong, we are able to come alongside them in a spirit of "me too" rather than "how could you?"

It grieves me deeply to think about the number of times I chose the latter, and disciplined my kids with a critical or judgmental spirit, because the shame I was living in was the shame I was living out. The voice of shame I heard in my head when I would get it wrong—the one that said, "What kind of mom does something like that? How could you?"—is the same language that overflowed into my parenting.

The language of shame equates what we do with the core of who we are. It makes hurtful and blanket statements. It relies on fear and anger to produce change in our children's hearts. It forgets the cross.

Here are just a few examples of the language of shame.

- How many times do I have to tell you this?

- How could you do something like that?

- What kind of kid does something like that?

- If only you were more like ...

- You should be ashamed of yourself.

  What else would you add to this list?

Has someone said similar things to you? Share how it impacted you.

When we throw shame at our children's failures, we create hopelessness in them. But grace! Grace inspires hope. Grace opens their hearts to repentance and transformation.

When we parent "broken together" we give our kids permission to take off their masks and let down their guards. We free them from feeling like they have to perform for our approval and obey perfectly for God's love. We liberate them from carrying secrets and suffering in silence—where shame festers.

Read Colossians 3:12-17. This passage is so full of wisdom on how to parent "broken together." I'd love for you to read these verses three times. And ask the Holy Spirit to illuminate the truths that He wants to show you specifically. Then write them below.

In verse 16, Paul exhorted us to *"Let the message about Christ, in all its richness, fill your lives."* In other words, let us immerse ourselves in the good news and experience the "broken together" overflow in our parenting. This approach with our kids sounds something more like this:

I know why you struggle with this. I know because I struggle, too. I get it. I get it because I need Jesus, too. Let's ask Him to forgive us and to help us with these struggles.

Read Hebrews 4:14-16. What did Jesus face? Yet He did not do what?

How are we to come before the throne of our gracious God?

What will we receive and find?

Having a "broken together" mind-set empowers us to come alongside our kids at the foot of the cross, and point them to the forgiving, rescuing, and transforming power of Christ. This mind-set empowers us to correct rather than condemn.

Rather than responding to their sin with shock, we respond with God's shocking love. And whichever one we choose will have a significant impact on our relationships with our children—and on our children's spirits.

In fact, the most sacred space to demonstrate God's love is in our children's failures. God demonstrated His love to us at our worst. To reflect His heart, we need to do the same with our children.

CLOSE WITH PRAYER
Father, thank You for Your healing and grace. Thank You for Your shocking love. Help me as I parent broken sinners as a broken sinner. I love You. Amen.

DAY 4

We are continuing our conversation from yesterday, so let's get right to it. We were looking at the blessing and benefits of parenting from a "broken together" place. And we have several more wonderful things to discover today.

Read Ephesians 4:1-3. The apostle Paul urged the Ephesians to do four things in verse 2. Note those four things below.

1.

2.

3.

4.

Sit with this for a moment and journal your thoughts below. If we made "every effort to keep the unity of the Spirit" (v. 3) in this way, what benefit would it have on our relationships with our kids?

Again, this is not a formula, and there are countless factors that can impact our relationships. But can we agree that when humility and gentleness and patience and loving forbearance is woven into our relationships with our kids, we are much more likely to have a warm relationships with our kids? Why is this so important? An insightful article by Kara Powell, at Fuller Youth Institute, revealed that "family warmth was more correlated with faith transmission than any other relational factor (including amount of contact between the generations, the type of contact, and the number of children in the family)."[2]

Did you catch that? What is more correlated with faith transmission than any other factor?

When we have warm relationships with our kids, we have unlimited potential for influence.

Family warmth occurs when our children feel accepted just as they are. When a strong sense of belonging permeates the homes. When we welcome them in their weaknesses, rather than withdraw from them. When not just our words, but our tone of voice and body language, emit warmth.

As noted by Kara Powell, there are five bad habits that can steal our family's warmth: "words, tone of voice, body language, technology, and fatigue."[3] Reading that list can be very convicting to us moms. Too often it's not my words that are the issue. It's my tone of voice or body language that builds walls between my kids and me. But here's the good news. It's never too late to change the temperature in our homes.

How does your thermostat read?

Do you think it's fair to say that moms under pressure are usually warmth killers? Why or why not?

What are some specific ways you can parent as a mom set free and increase warmth in your home?

When we have family warmth, our kids are more likely to be open to receiving the seeds of faith we desire to plant in their hearts—seeds such as prayer, reading the Bible, Scripture memorization, worship, and service. These seeds—or spiritual disciplines—not only enrich their knowledge of Jesus but also lead to a deeper relationship with Him. They help our children trust Jesus as their Savior, worship Him as their Lord, experience Him as their best friend, and discover He is the truest satisfaction of their souls. And through these seeds, the Holy Spirit's sanctifying power is unleashed in our children's lives.

Planting seeds of faith in our kids' hearts is another way we make the good news central in our homes. So I want to briefly talk about these seeds with you.

But before we go there, we have to go to the no-guilt zone, OK? Because I don't know a single mom who doesn't already feel like she isn't doing enough when it comes to nurturing her child's faith.

For example, when I traveled to Alabama to speak at a parenting conference last year I stayed with one of my dearest friends, Tamara, who also happened to be my college roommate. It was such fun to spend a weekend with her and her sweet family. Well, the morning of the event, I grabbed a cup of coffee and joined Tamara and her four children in their living room where they were doing their morning devotions. They concluded their devotion time by reciting the Book of James. From memory. No, that wasn't a typo. *The entire Book of James.* From memory.

He knows our hearts better than we do.

Meanwhile, my boys had memorized a mere two— (one, two, the end)—verses that summer. Can you imagine the way the enemy tried to use that against me right before I spoke at a parenting event about raising kids with a vibrant faith? Oh, yes he did.

The mom who has her kids memorize the Book of James and the mom who only memorized two verses with her kids and the mom who is still trying to figure out how to just read the Bible with her kids and hasn't memorized a single verse at all each probably feel like they could be and should be doing so much more.

So this conversation isn't going to a be a guilt trip. It's going to be an invitation. An invitation to do the next best thing to grow closer to Jesus alongside our kids. Deal?

There is so very much I want to say about each one of these seeds but for the sake of time, we will focus on prayer and reading God's Word.

PLANTING THE SEED OF PRAYER

We've talked about the significance of this for our own lives and our parenting, but now let's apply it to our kids. Our children need to know that no request is too big, no sin is too bad, no shame is too great, and no feeling is too unworthy to bring to God in prayer. He knows our hearts even better than we do, which means we aren't telling Him anything He doesn't already know.

Read and record what the following three verses tell us about the way God knows our hearts.

> The LORD searches every heart and understands the intention of every thought. If you seek him, he will be found by you.
> 1 CHRONICLES 28:9b

> And God, who knows the heart, bore witness to them by giving them the Holy Spirit, just as he also did to us.
> ACTS 15:8

> No creature is hidden from him, but all things are naked and exposed to the eyes of him to whom we must give an account.
> HEBREWS 4:13

God knows the heart. This frees our children to come to their heavenly Father with their hopes and dreams, their struggles and sorrows, and even their fears and doubts.

> One of my favorite ways to pray as a family is with the four words *wow, sorry, thanks,* and *please.*

> *Wow:* We adore Jesus for who He is and what He has done for us.

> *Sorry:* We confess our sin and we receive His forgiveness.

> *Thanks:* We thank Jesus for who we are in Him and for everything He has given us.

> *Please:* We present our requests and we receive His peace.

Prayer is getting real with Jesus, not telling Him what we think He wants to hear. We never have to fear His rejection or His disappointment. He loves it when we pray, and He desires to hear what we have to say.

What obstacles keep you from praying with your children?

What are some ways you can incorporate prayer into daily life with your kids?

STUDYING GOD'S WORD

The other seed of faith I want us to explore briefly is God's Word. The greatest gift we can give our kids when it comes to the Bible is teaching them that it's not primarily about us and what we should be doing. It's not a collection of morality tales and to-do lists and fictional super heroes. The Bible is the infallible Word of God. It's about God and what He has already done for us through Christ Jesus. It's the truest story ever told—the story of our Savior, Jesus Christ, who loved us enough to leave His throne in heaven to lay down His life to rescue us, redeem us, and reunite us with our Father. Reading the Bible through that lens changes everything.

Read the following verses and record the benefits of planting the seed of God's Word in our kids' hearts.

For the word of God is living and effective and sharper than any double-edged sword, penetrating as far as the separation of soul and spirit, joints and marrow. It is able to judge the thoughts and intentions of the heart.
HEBREWS 4:12

God's Word is _____.

prayer is getting real with Jesus, not telling Him what we think He wants to hear.

Your word is a lamp for my feet and a light on my path.
PSALM 119:105

God's Word gives _____.

So my word that comes from my mouth will not return to me empty, but it will accomplish what I please and will prosper in what I send it to do.
ISAIAH 55:11

God's Word will _____.

All Scripture is inspired by God and is profitable for teaching, for rebuking, for correcting, for training in righteousness, so that the man of God may be complete, equipped for every good work.
2 TIMOTHY 3:16-17

God's Word equips us for _____.

What obstacles do you encounter when trying to guide your kids in reading God's Word?

What one next step can you take to make God's Word more central in your daily lives?

Studying God's Word as a family is essential to making the good news central in our homes and leading our children in discovering the heart of our heavenly Father.

CLOSE WITH PRAYER

Lord, help me as I seek to increase the warmth in my home. I pray that You would show me new ways to lead my children in prayer and reading Your Word. Guide my family to know and love You more each day.

There is one last piece of encouragement I want to give to you.

We've spent the week looking at some of the ways we can make the gospel central in our homes. We've discovered how—as we remember who we are in Christ and the grace that has us covered as parents—we are inspired and empowered to be a vessel of that grace to our kids. And we are ready to see grace transform our hearts and homes.

But, I want to make sure our shoulders aren't once again heavy with burdens we aren't meant to carry. I want to ensure we haven't picked up things we've been freed to lay down. And to do so, I want to share with you a recent conversation I had with a good friend.

I was wrestling with how to give my kids grace in a difficult situation, so I gave my friend Jessica a call. Though we are similar in age, she has very much been a mentor to me. The way she shares the good news speaks directly to my heart.

We are ready to see grace transform our hearts and homes.

After we spent about thirty minutes talking through my questions and were preparing to hang up the phone, I could tell Jessica felt my remaining angst. Though I was no longer feeling the pressure to be a perfect mom who was raising perfect kids, I was still feeling the pressure to give grace perfectly to my kids.

So before we hung up, Jessica gave me one last piece of advice, and it was some of the most freeing advice I've ever been given.

"Jeannie," she gently said, "the way you give your kids the gospel isn't going to determine whether or not they accept it. It's not all on you."

Do you see how she framed the significance of my role in light of God's sovereignty?

In other words, yes, absolutely make every effort to make the gospel central in your home and give your kids grace. But please don't carry the pressure of thinking that if you always give it to them the "right" way, they will come to love Jesus more, and if you always give it to them the "wrong" way, they will not come to love Jesus at all. God is good at using our weaknesses to show His power.

So my dear fellow mom, will you repeat these truths with me?

- I am significant in my kid's lives, but I am not sovereign. God is.

- I can trust God with the children He has entrusted to me.

- My job isn't to be the perfection of Christ. It's to point my children to Christ— the only One who has never and will never let them down.

- I can lay down what God has not asked me to carry so I can thrive in what He has.

- God's grace is magnified in my weakness, and I am free from the pressure to get it all right.

- I can rely on the power of Christ in me.

- I don't have to be enough because Christ in me already is.

- And absolutely nothing can separate me from the love of Christ.

CLOSE WITH PRAYER
Write your prayers to God as you pray by name for your children.

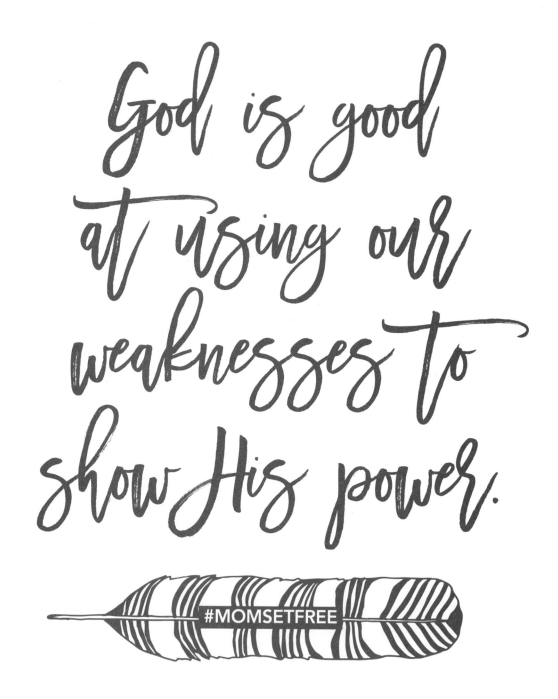

God is good at using our weaknesses to show His power.

#MOMSETFREE

PARENTING IN FREEDOM

Group Discussion Questions

1. Review the chart on page 105 that contrasts who we are in the flesh versus who we are in Christ. Why is seeing the truth of who we are with and without Christ so important for our kids?

2. What are some practical ways you anchor your children's identities in Christ? How do you foster "Christ-worth" in their lives?

3. How did this week's study help you identify places where shame might be woven into your parenting? How can you replace shame-full messages with grace-full truth?

4. How does saying "me too" with your children and acknowledging your failures and weaknesses, set your kids free to be honest about their failures and weaknesses?

5. Read Romans 2:4. How are you reflecting God's heart with your children? In what ways is that transforming you and them?

6. Share unique ways you plant "seeds of faith" in your kids' hearts to make the gospel central in your parenting.

_____

_____

_____

_____

To hear more from Jeannie,
download the optional video
bundle at lifeway.com/momsetfree

Well, my friend, I can barely believe it but here we are at Week 6. We are on the home stretch of our journey to parenting as a mom set free. This week is going to entail a whole lot of practical application for parenting with grace. We are going to dispel some common myths around parenting with grace and wrap up our journey with knowledge and tools to make grace reverberate throughout our homes every day in practical ways. Before we do, I feel compelled to tell you this again—I, by no means, have all the answers. A challenging and complicated situation with my son, just last night, reminded me of this reality. I'm still learning alongside you, dear mom. But I do want to share with you some of the things God has been teaching me. Ready?

"Mom, come on. Give us some grace. Pleeeeassse." That was my son Brennan's plea when I corrected my boys over the way they were treating each other on a Saturday evening in the backyard.

Maybe your kids have pulled the "grace card" too when they've disobeyed and know consequences are imminent. Well, this is precisely why I am so excited about what we are going to study this week, because Brennan's plea reflects a common misunderstanding about grace. So let's start here, by answering, *What is parenting with grace?*

This is a big question on which all the others rest. And to answer it, I think we may be best served by looking, first, at what parenting with grace is not.

- It's not ignoring or excusing our children's sin.

- It's not turning a blind eye to their behavior or giving them a free pass to sin or do as they please.

- It's not the absence of establishing rules, boundaries, consistency, consequences, or discipline in our parenting.

- It does not make obedience optional for our children.

   What other things would you add to this list?

So what *is* parenting with grace?

- It's weaving the good news of Jesus Christ into how we establish our authority, require obedience, train, and discipline our kids.

- It's reflecting God's heart of unconditional love and forgiveness when we address our children's sin and weaknesses.

- It's remembering that when God disciplines us, He doesn't rely on a pointed finger, an angry tone, and a shameful message to convict our hearts and inspire obedience. Instead, He is rushing in to rescue us from our sin and redirect us to the path that leads to life. To parent with grace is to do the same.

  Reflect and record how a "rescue and redirect" approach reflects God's heart to our kids.

READ ROMANS 2:4.

The Message translation reads, *"God is kind, but he's not soft. In kindness he takes us firmly by the hand and leads us into a radical life-change."*

What does this passage reveal about the way God parents us?

Parenting from a framework of grace means leading our children in the same way that Romans 2:4 says God leads us. God isn't soft, but He is kind. He is firm, but He is also gentle. He puts His hand in ours and leads us into a transformed, God-glorifying, freedom-full way of life. It's God's kindness and patience, not His wrath and fury, that turns us toward repentance, transformation, and obedience.

To reflect God's heart, the message for our kids is: I require obedience *from* you because I'm for you. And I want you to reap the benefits of staying on the path that leads to life and enjoying the pleasures that come with pursuing holiness—not fleeting worldly pleasures but something so much greater. I want you to experience the incomparable adventure that comes with putting your faith in God and being used by Him in His redemptive narrative. I recognize that obedience does not come naturally to our rebellious hearts. Obedience requires sacrifice and effort and discipline, but don't lose sight of this—there is tremendous freedom that flows from obedience. Freedom from guilt and shame and regret.

Read Proverbs 3:1-6. What does this passage tell us about the benefits of trusting the Lord and keeping His commands?

Read Galatians 6:7-8. What happens when we don't trust God and keep His commands?

In Galatians 6, Paul taught about consequences. For instance, when we sow seeds of dishonesty and insincerity, we will reap a harvest of mistrust, guilt, and hypocrisy. I'm not referring to the karmic "what goes around comes around" system of payback, which is in complete contradiction to grace, but simply acknowledging that our choices do indeed have consequences. Even if we escape the worldly ramifications of a certain situation, our hearts know the truth. And little by little, the choices we make will either edify or wreak havoc in our lives (Mark 8:36).

We know the importance of teaching our children that there are consequences to their actions. But when we teach this reality to our kids, it's even more important for our children to understand another truth: Simple cause and effect in our human interactions is not true of our life before God. God is not keeping score and ensuring that the consequences flow in direct proportion to the offense. As we read in **PSALM 103:8-10,** *"The LORD is compassionate and gracious, slow to anger and abounding in faithful love. He will not always accuse us or be angry forever. He has not dealt with us as our sins deserve or repaid us according to our iniquities."*

If we want to parent with grace, the question we have to continually ask ourselves is "How can I reflect God's heart in the way I train and discipline my kids in this situation?" That is a great starting place.

Reflect on a recent experience with your kids in which asking yourself this question would have changed how you parented them.

What simple step or change can you make today to help you keep this question in the forefront of your mind—how can I reflect God's heart in the way I train and discipline my kids?

If the enemy is using this exercise to throw shame at your mistakes, stop here and remember God's grace for you. Remember the Holy Spirit convicts us and leads us to repentance. The enemy condemns us and leads us to shame.

How might God be inviting you to receive His mercy?

How can I reflect God's heart in the way I train and discipline my kids?

This leads us to another myth regarding parenting with grace, which is that it can be "too late" for us to give our kids grace and do things differently now.

I was recently with a beautiful girl in her mid-20s who was reflecting on how the tumultuous way she was parented influenced many of the poor decisions she made. She went on to say, "But several months ago, my parents invited my siblings and me for dinner. And that evening, we all sat in the living room while my mom and dad apologized and asked for our forgiveness. They confessed the many mistakes they'd made and the lack of unconditional love they showed. It was one of the most powerful and healing moments in my life, and my siblings felt the same. We know they did the best they knew how to do, and while we all suffered from some of their mistakes, we all see how God's hand was on each of us through it all."

Her story was an important reminder that whether we are in the early stages of our parenting journey or our kids have long ago left the house and started families of their own, if we still have breath, we can still say something like: "This parenting thing can be hard and confusing, and I don't always know what I'm doing. So I want to say I'm sorry for the times I have not reflected God's heart to you. I'd give anything to go back and get less wrong and get more right. I'm just beginning to understand what grace means. I've had a hard time accepting God's unconditional love for me in all of my weaknesses and failures, so it's been very hard for me to show you God's love for you at times. But I want to do it differently, and with God's help, and by God's grace, I will. Please forgive me."

Based on your own personal journey and the ages of your children, take a moment to write the words God might be inviting you to share with your children.

I can tell you this. It wasn't long ago that I found myself creeping back toward perfectionist parenting. I saw all the warning signs. Getting too angry too quickly. Saying "I don't expect perfection" but acting like I did. Being more critical and less joyful. And I felt God inviting me to talk honestly with my eldest son about it. That day just so happened to be a day in which my other boys were headed off to sports with other friends after school, so I was alone with Cal in the car. As we were driving home, I asked Cal, "Hey buddy. My heart has been very convicted about something, and I want to talk to you about it. Is that OK?"

"Of course, mom. What's up?" he said.

"Well, I think I've been putting a lot of pressure on you lately to be perfect and I haven't been doing a very good job of reflecting God's heart of grace to you. And I want you to always feel free to tell me when I am doing that. I want you to be able to be honest with me when I'm making you feel like you have to be perfect."

My beautiful son felt free to share his heart with me in that moment. He told me he did feel the pressure. But when I invited him to be honest with me, I saw relief in his eyes, and I sensed the weight roll off his back. We both remembered grace.

It's never too late to give our kids grace, because it's never too late to give love. We don't have to be afraid to be vulnerable with our kids about this. Remember, we can be "broken together."

CLOSE WITH PRAYER

Lord, help me to discipline my children in light of Your grace and love. Give me boldness to admit my weaknesses and failures. Help them to see Your love through me. Amen.

DAY 2

Today we are going to pick right back up where we left off yesterday looking at some of the common myths around parenting with grace.

The first myth I want us to look at is that grace and discipline have to be "balanced." I've often heard the question asked, "How do I know when to give grace or to give discipline?" So today I want to propose a different question. What if, instead, we asked, "How can I weave grace into my discipline?" Because I believe grace and discipline can coexist. It doesn't have to be one or the other. Grace is the unconditional love of God woven into our discipline.

> READ PROVERBS 3:11-12 (NIV):
> *My son, do not despise the LORD's discipline, and do not resent his rebuke, because the LORD disciplines those he loves, as a father the son he delights in.*
>
> What does the Lord do for those He loves?
>
> Read Hebrews 12:4-12. While this passage echoes Proverbs 3, what else does it reveal about God's discipline?
>
>
>
> Now look specifically at verse 10. God disciplines for our
> _____, in order that we may share in His _____.

Grace in discipline is corrective and instructional, and it is for our children's good. We want our kids to understand that the commandments and promises of Christ are gifts we give them—gifts that set them free to live into the purpose for which they were so wonderfully created.

> How does thinking about the commandments and promises of Christ as gifts we give our kids change how you might approach discipline?

Our kids need—and want—us to be consistent in discipline. Our 2-year-old and our 17-year-old need us to establish healthy boundaries and consequences and be consistent in enforcing them. Our kids need to know that we say what we mean and we mean what we say, even though they'll definitely never admit it. Right? I mean, when was the last time your child came to you and said, "Hey mom, I really need you to be consistent with boundaries and consequences, so I know I can count on you and learn to rely on God to make wise choices in the future." Exactly! Me neither. Though let us not confuse consistent with stringent. If we overreact and give them a consequence that doesn't fit the crime, or if we are unreasonable when they want to explain their actions, or if we are inflexible in a situation that could have used a little mercy, it's OK for us to back up and say, "I got that wrong, and I want to make it right."

What keeps you from being consistent with discipline? What ramifications can this have on your kids?

Still, we must remember that giving our kids clear rules, consistent boundaries, and logical consequences may change their outward behavior, but only the grace of God can lead them to repentance or bring lasting transformation of their hearts.

How does knowing that only God can lead your children to repentance change how you discipline your kids?

Today we will see how we have the privilege of being included in the work God is doing in our kids' lives as we rely on Him to transform their hearts. How awesome is that? I'll use an example of something that recently went down in our house.

I was in my bedroom getting ready for the day, and I could hear two of my boys in their bathroom doing the same. They were going about their usual business when, very quickly, their voices started escalating and their harsh words started flying. I knew it was only a matter of seconds before the offended son would be in my room, crying and shouting about how his brother "always" takes advantage of him and "never" treats him fairly.

I usually require that my boys work these arguments out on their own with the problem-solving/peace-making skills my husband and I have taught them, but I could already tell this situation was going nowhere good, and fast, so it needed my intervention.

I called the boys into my room and asked them to tell me what happened, and they each proceeded to explain that this fight was essentially over a hairbrush. This went on for several minutes when, finally, the offender son halted the conversation and exclaimed with great frustration, "Are we really spending this much time talking about a hairbrush?"

I smiled. I waited. And then I responded, "I'm so glad you asked that question." The look on my son's face told me he already knew where this was headed because "heart-talks" happen often in our home.

"No buddy, this isn't about the hairbrush at all. This is about what was going on inside your heart when you yanked that brush out of his hand and when you both proceeded to hurt each other with your angry words. So let's talk about that."

A heart-talk is just one way we weave grace into our parenting and make the gospel central in our homes. It involves walking our kids through four simple words—*What, Why, How,* and *Now.* Every heart-talk doesn't have to include Scripture reading with our kids, but we should regularly point our children to the Bible as the foundation of learning how to be Christlike. Let's walk through a few examples together.

1. WHAT WAS GOING ON IN YOUR HEART?
Said simply, God cares about the heart.

READ: Matthew 15:3-20

THEME: "Their heart is far from me" (v. 8) and "what comes out of the mouth comes from the heart" (v. 18).

Asking "What was going on in your heart?" helps our children identify the belief of the heart that overflows into the behavior. Because, really, that's what it means to focus on our child's heart. Belief motivates behavior, and it's important for our kids to make that connection. Proverbs and the Gospel of Luke point us to this idea of heart overflow.

READ: Proverbs 4:23; Luke 6:45

What wise instruction do these verses provide?

This question requires our children to think about more than just the outward behavior they displayed and reminds them of the importance of guarding their heart. It requires them to think about what they feed their heart: *Are you feeding your heart with the truth and power of God's Word? What are you watching? What are you listening to? Who are you spending time with? What are you reading?*

This gives children the opportunity to confess that their actions have been selfishly motivated. My son realized he was only thinking about getting what he wanted, when he wanted it. He also confessed that his actions lacked kindness, as he did not treat his brother as he would want to be treated.

If and when your kids are not willing to come clean, may I offer you just one idea to guide them in truth? When this happens in our family, I instruct my boys with something like, "I want you to be honest so you don't carry the guilt that comes with lying. And I want you to remember that whatever you did wrong has already been forgiven and paid for in Jesus. Ask God to give you a heart that desires honesty. This is not a house of perfection, but confession." I am by no means suggesting that this is a formula that fixes everything every time. Grace is not a formula. But grace most often frees our children to confess the things that fear or shame were preventing them from disclosing. That's what grace does. Which leads us nicely into the "why."

2. WHY DID YOU DO WHAT YOU DID?
The beauty of this question is that the answer ultimately points us back to Jesus. And it reminds us to parent "broken together."

READ: Ecclesiastes 7:20; Jeremiah 17:9; Romans 7:15-25

THEME: We are sinners in need of a Savior, and a Savior we do indeed have in Jesus Christ. This is not excusing or endorsing the sin but acknowledging the reality of our fallen human nature. It's acknowledging that our hearts are prone to wander and rebel and inclined to selfish desires and wants. We're not inviting our kids to hide behind an "Oh well, we're imperfect" excuse. Instead, by remembering that God takes sin (very) seriously, we become more grateful for our Savior.

3. HOW COULD YOU HAVE OBEYED GOD IN THAT SITUATION?

This question invites us to train our children in the Lord's instruction.

THEME: Work together to come up with the words your children could have used or the behavior they could have had in the situation.

If your kids are on the younger side, you can role-play the how. This is highly effective in training. Have them start at the beginning and walk back through the situation with the right attitude and actions.

This is also a great opportunity to recall Bible verses with our children. Grab a Bible and turn to your concordance to review Scripture passages on each of the fruit of the Spirit. Or look up a few verses that provide guidance on the very sin or disobedience your child is struggling with.

READ: 2 Timothy 3:16-17

And most beautifully, this part of the conversation is also an awesome opportunity to remember we need the Holy Spirit to produce the fruit of the Spirit in our lives. We can't obey God's law without the power of God's Spirit.

READ: 2 Thessalonians 1:11-12

> We are obedient through whose power? For whose glory?

We are going to talk more about how to guide our children in relying on the Holy Spirit on Day 4, so let's keep going.

4. NOW, THE CONSEQUENCE.

This part of the conversation addresses the consequence, although there may not always be some big grand consequence. Sometimes the consequence is the conversation itself. In walking our kids through the *what, why, how,* and *now* process, the Holy Spirit convicts their hearts, they experience genuine repentance, and the work is done.

This is typically when I offer our kids what I call a "mercy moment."

READ: Psalm 103:10-14

Just as the Lord has shown extravagant mercy to us, we can show mercy to our kids.

READ: Lamentations 3:20-24

> How can we incorporate the truth we find in Lamentations into our parenting to point our kids to Christ?

However, when their behavior does require a consequence (and oftentimes it does), let us remember the love with which God disciplines us. In doing so, we guard against allowing our anger to overflow into our discipline.

By using these four simple words—*what, why, how,* and *now*—we can train and discipline our children in a way that shifts our focus from forcing change in their outward behavior to reaching their hearts with God's truth and grace. Because, while we do not have the responsibility or ability to transform our child's heart, we can help them understand what's going on inside of it.

CLOSE WITH PRAYER

Father, thank You for entrusting me with these children. Help me to reflect Your heart as I disciple and discipline them. Amen.

DAY 3

OK friend, today we are talking about anger. We are talking about our tempers and our lack of patience and our short fuses. I know few moms who don't struggle with anger in their parenting, and this topic has been taboo for too long. We've been afraid to confess this is a weakness in our lives because we fear we're the only ones who struggle with it. Every other mom looks so patient at the playground when her kid throws a temper tantrum. Most moms use their gentle voice in public, so we assume they'd never roar like lions behind closed doors. Oh, yes, it's time to talk about this. It's time to talk honestly about the danger of anger and beg the Holy Spirit to do some serious work in our hearts.

We're going to look at several passages that provide guidance around anger. But here's the thing. Reading with our eyes and knowing in our minds what Scripture tells us to do with our anger does not provide the power to actually do it.

For example, I know the passages we are about to explore by memory, and yet, there are a lot of days when I jump right into the chaos and throw a temper tantrum of my own. There are plenty of days when:

- my anger and sinful nature win;

- I threaten when I should listen; and

- I react instead of respond.

In other words, every single day (every single hour) requires that I look to Christ, remember I am a new creation in Him, and live from that identity, by the power of the Holy Spirit.

We cannot do this on our own.

OK, are you ready?

> Read James 1:19-25.

What three things does verse 19 tell us to do?

What does verse 20 assure us anger does not produce?

God's perfect law provides us freedom and blessing.

In the NIV translation, verse 25 reads, *"But whoever looks intently into the perfect law that gives freedom, and continues in it—not forgetting what they have heard, but doing it—they will be blessed in what they do."*

God's perfect law provides us freedom and blessing.

So many of my parenting regrets are the result of me not heeding this wisdom. Indeed, I've never seen my anger produce repentance and righteousness in my kids. Only shame and sadness. My anger has never produced freedom and blessing in my own life. Only regret and grief.

READ GALATIANS 6:1-2:
Brothers and sisters, if someone is overtaken in any wrongdoing, you who are spiritual, restore such a person with a gentle spirit, watching out for yourselves so that you also won't be tempted. Carry one another's burdens; in this way you will fulfill the law of Christ.

Fill in the blanks:

If our child is caught in sin, we—who are _____ should restore them with a _____ spirit.

We need to be dependent on the Holy Spirit to correct gently. How easy is it for us to also fall into sin in the way we correct our kids—be it through anger, shame, or fear tactics? Too easy.

Paul was exhorting us to fulfill the law of Christ by doing what with our children's burdens?

We're called to carry each other's burdens—right to the cross. Sounds a lot like a "broken together" approach, doesn't it?

READ COLOSSIANS 3:21:
Fathers, do not exasperate your children, so that they won't become discouraged.

The Message translation reads: *"Parents, don't come down too hard on your children or you'll crush their spirits."*

Oh, this is so important. What's becoming more and more clear to me is that making our kids feel bad won't make them want to be good. It just drives them deeper into despair. Rather than coming down on them in anger or shame, we must come alongside them in grace.

Think about a recent situation when you reacted in anger. How could you have reacted differently by coming alongside your child in grace?

Remember, the grace is for you, too. Pause here to pray, asking and thanking God for forgiveness in this situation.

READ EPHESIANS 6:4 (NLT):
Fathers, do not provoke your children to anger by the way you treat them. Rather, bring them up with the discipline and instruction that comes from the Lord.

If we twist Scripture to get our children to obey, if we hammer them over the head with the commandments of God, or if we provoke them to anger because we lash out with our own, we have not brought them up in the discipline and instruction of the Lord.

The discipline and instruction that comes from the Lord is grounded in love. Remember, while their choices may require correction and consequences, *"there is now no condemnation for those in Christ Jesus"* **(ROM. 8:1).**

> **How does correction in our parenting look different than condemnation?**

Now, I'm not saying that it's wrong to feel anger. I'm reminded of **EPHESIANS 4:26** in which the apostle Paul writes, *"Be angry and do not sin."* See, there is a difference in sinful anger and righteous anger, which I think is worth noting before we move on.

Righteous anger is essentially being angry about the things that make God angry. John Bloom writes,

> Righteous anger doesn't look or feel like sinful anger because godly righteous anger is governed and directed by love. God is righteous, but he is also love (1 John 4:8). And love is patient (1 Corinthians 13:4). That's why God repeatedly describes himself in Scripture as "merciful and gracious, slow to anger, and abounding in steadfast love and faithfulness" (Exodus 34:6; Numbers 14:18; Nehemiah 9:17; Psalm 86:15; 103:8; 145:8; Joel 2:13; Jonah 4:2; Nahum 1:3). ... Being angry and not sinning requires the discernment of constant practice (Hebrews 5:14) because so much of our anger *is* rooted in our prideful, selfish sin nature. ... We will never be perfectly angry in this age. But we can grow in the grace of righteous anger. God means us to. It is part of being conformed to the image of Christ (Romans 8:2).[1]

Moms, to be conformed to the image of Christ and reflect His heart in our parenting, we must surrender any right we feel we have to sinful anger—to act harshly and unkindly to our kids. And we do this by first remembering God's kindness to us in Jesus Christ.

When I fail to be kind, gentle, and patient with my kids, it's because I've forgotten how kind, patient, and gentle God has been to me in Christ.

Are we seeing how becoming a better, more grace-filled mom doesn't happen by merely trying harder? It happens by more deeply believing the gospel for ourselves.

Remembering the mercy, kindness, and patience of God for us frees us from being stuck in anger and empowers us to parent with gentleness and self-control.

> READ PSALM 37:4-8 (NLT):
> *4 Take delight in the LORD, and he will give you your heart's desires. 5 Commit everything you do to the LORD. Trust him, and he will help you. 6 He will make your innocence radiate like the dawn, and the justice of your cause will shine like the noonday sun. 7 Be still in the presence of the LORD, and wait patiently for him to act. Don't worry about evil people who prosper or fret about their wicked schemes. 8 Stop being angry! Turn from your rage! Do not lose your temper—it only leads to harm.*

I just know that your heart desires to be gentle and self-controlled with your kids.

Read verse 4 again and fill in the blanks below, because the psalmist gave very clear guidance on how we can have what our hearts desire.

Verse 4: "_____ _____ _____ _____ _____, and he will give you your heart's desires."

Verse 5: Commit everything you do to the LORD. Trust him, and he will _____ _____.

Record any other thoughts God is laying on your heart about this passage for your parenting.

Now let's make this practical. Here are three very simple ways we can heed the psalmist's instruction and turn from our rage before we lose it on our kids.

1. DON'T DO ANYTHING IN THE HEAT OF THE MOMENT. I used to think I had to deal with every little grievance right on the spot. But I've learned it's OK to say, *I need a time-out. I need to take this to Jesus. I'll get back to you on this, because I can't be who I need to be at this moment.*

Yes, you can take a time-out. And when you do, ask Jesus to help you remember your own brokenness and equip you with resurrection power to fight your sinful nature. In doing this, we model for our kids how to respond rather than react.

2. PRAY—RIGHT THERE, RIGHT THEN. When I find myself on the verge of yelling at my kids, you know what I try to do? Yell out to God instead. I'm not kidding. It sounds like: *Lord, this is an emergency. I need You and I need You now. I'm angry, and I know I'm not honoring You or obeying You when I come down on my kids. Please help me right now.*

Perhaps I sound crazy to you and look nuts to my kids, but I'm OK looking nuts for Jesus. It seems like a better choice than going nuts on my kids. And it teaches our kids to take anything, at any time, to Jesus.

3. ENVISION THE CROSS BETWEEN YOU AND YOUR CHILD. I am a visual person. Tell me something, I forget it. Show me something, it's with me for life. So what I've found to be incredibly helpful is literally envisioning a cross between my child and me, because shame, anger, and fear tactics can't penetrate the cross. If the cross of Christ is between my child and me, there are only two ways to get to the other side. I either choose to go around the cross and discipline in my sinful nature, or I choose to go through the cross and discipline in grace. There's a choice to be made. Choosing to put the cross between us—seeing our children through the lens of the self-giving love of Christ—is how we make the good news central in our homes.

> Can you think of a recent situation in which envisioning the cross between your child and you would have changed your response? What did you do?

> What would you have done differently?

> What other ways have you been able to "be angry and ... not sin"?

Today's homework was not easy, my friend. And lest the enemy tempt us to despair as we've faced this tough topic, let us remember grace as we wrap up. May I encourage you with this: On the days when you fail to respond with grace—like when you throw a temper tantrum that rivals theirs, or you throw shame at their failure, or you throw empty threats and fear tactics around like confetti—you can remember the grace that is available to you in that very moment, lavishly poured out on you when you fail. You can welcome His grace, be led to repentance, seek your child's forgiveness, and surrender—again—to the Holy Spirit's transforming power in your own heart.

We want our parenting to be marked with compassion and self-control. We want to be firm but gentle. No-nonsense but nurturing. So let's close today with Psalm 139:23-24, and invite God to do His good work in us.

> *Search me, O God, and know my heart!*
> *Try me and know my thoughts! And see if*
> *there be any grievous way in me, and lead*
> *me in the way everlasting!*
> **PSALM 139:23-24, ESV**

May God seal in our hearts all we've learned and give us a fresh tenderness in our interactions with our children.

CLOSE WITH PRAYER
Use Psalm 139:23-24 to write a short prayer of response to God.

Grace is available to you, lavishly poured out on you.

You are amazing! Truly. You may have missed a few days or even a few weeks of our study, but you kept going. I'm so grateful. And though we are coming to the end of journeying together through this study, this is only just the beginning of the good work God is going to do in our hearts and in our parenting.

So to wrap up our study time together, I want us to answer one final question that I find most moms have about parenting with grace: "What if my kids take advantage of grace?" If this is a remaining fear or worry of yours, I first want to say welcome to the club. We moms naturally worry that our kids will abuse or misuse the grace we give them, and that it will ultimately backfire on us. Is that fair to say?

As one mom said to me not long ago, "I want to give my kids grace, but I'm too afraid to 'try it' because I don't think it 'will work' on my kids. You'd know what I mean if you knew my kids. They'll steamroll me if I let up on the rules and give them grace."

Ah. And there it was. Her fear was mostly rooted in a misunderstanding of what it means to parent with grace. And, as we continued to chat, she revealed that she was still struggling to know the grace of God herself.

Again, this is why the work we did in Week 3 and Week 4 was so critical to our journey of living—and parenting—as a mom set free. Because when you've personally tasted grace, and you've experienced it's sweetness, you know—that you know—that grace is what actually inspires you to turn from sin because you can barely believe the extent to which God went to rescue you from the wages of it.

There's only one thing that has the power to help us overcome sin and ungodliness, and Paul tells us what that is in this letter he wrote to Titus.

>   Read Titus 2:11-14.

Grace is portrayed as our teacher here, and what it teaches us is to say no to sin and yes to godliness. Grace ignites gratitude in our hearts, and gratitude enlivens obedience to God. But does this mean we should ignore God's law and only give our kids God's grace?

READ ROMANS 7:12:

So then, the law is holy, and the commandment is holy and just and good.

How is the law described by Paul?

READ ROMANS 3:19-20:

Now we know that whatever the law says, it speaks to those who are subject to the law, so that every mouth may be shut and the whole world may become subject to God's judgment. For no one will be justified in his sight by the works of the law, because the knowledge of sin comes through the law.

What does Paul say the law is intended to do?

God's law shows us how to live and makes us conscious of our sin. God's grace, by the power of the Holy Spirit, inspires us to live in obedience to the law.

Both are essential in the Christian life. But what we have to know—what we must know—is that giving our kids God's law and telling our kids how to live does not enable or equip them to do it. Our hearts are not inspired to obedience merely because God said so. Our hearts are inspired to obedience because Jesus already did so. Knowing how Jesus perfectly obeyed the "rules" on their behalf inspires gratitude. And gratitude for God's grace is the greatest motivator for godliness.

The *ESV Gospel Transformation Bible* frames it so beautifully this way.

> "Self-controlled, upright, and godly lives ... zealous for good works" are produced by embracing the grace of God. ... A profound encounter with the grace of the gospel is the only thing that can produce change at the level of our *desires*. The gospel produces such loving and longing for our great God and Savior Jesus Christ that we desire to honor him with our lives (v. 13). When that love and longing are present, godly behaviors follow.[2]

Let me give you a personal example. When I first became a mom, I was given the wonderful advice to choose a Bible verse that would serve as our family mission statement—a verse that would reflect what's most important to us and would guide us in our decision-making as a family.

I loved the idea, and I didn't have to think long about which verse to choose because I had a very clear picture of what I wanted to create—a home with God-loving and God-obeying kids. Therefore, the greatest commandment, which we read together in Week 2 (p. 51), was my obvious and immediate choice. Our family mission statement would be to love the Lord our God with all our heart and love our neighbor as ourselves (see Matt. 22:37-39).

To accompany our family mission statement, I made a long list of house rules for godly growth—which was essentially a list of Christlike virtues. I posted it on our refrigerator and got busy trying to produce the fruit of the Spirit in my kids' lives. Along with each virtue, I listed a Bible verse or two, so I could refer to God's Word when instructing them.

But here's the thing. What I didn't understand back then is that Bible verses posted on bulletin boards wouldn't produce in my kids' hearts a love for God and a desire to obey His Word. Only gratitude for God's grace does that! And it was only as I began to understand this truth that I stopped worrying my kids would take advantage of grace. In fact, grace became the very thing on which I hung all my hope.

Therefore, our family mission statement is still the greatest commandment. But it's not my starting place with my kids. Here's my starting place:

> *I pray that from his glorious, unlimited resources he will empower you with inner strength through his Spirit. Then Christ will make his home in your hearts as you trust in him. Your roots will grow down into God's love and keep you strong. And may you have the power to understand, as all God's people should, how wide, how long, how high, and how deep his love is. May you experience the love of Christ, though it is too great to understand fully. Then you will be made complete with all the fullness of life and power that comes from God.*
> EPHESIANS 3:16-19, NLT

This is the verse I pray with my kids every single morning. Because they need to know His love before they will desire to obey His law.

Do you have a family mission statement or verse? If so, what is it? If not, take a moment now to reflect on what you'd want it to include.

So to wrap up, I want us to look at three practical ways we can nurture gratitude for God's grace in our kid's hearts on a daily basis using these three words: *remember, rely,* and *recognize.*

1. REMEMBER WHAT JESUS HAS ALREADY DONE FOR THEM.
Before asking our children to respond as Jesus would, let's first help them remember what Jesus has already done.

Now, if you're anything like me, reminding your children of what Jesus has done wouldn't necessarily be your natural response. Instead, your first instinct might be to point out what your children did wrong and then throw in a Bible verse, for good measure, to show them how to do it right, right? (And sometimes that's all we can do with the time or bandwidth we've got, and that's OK, too.) But let's also take a look at a few examples of how we can help our children to first remember what Jesus has already done, and then instruct them how to respond as He would.

When our children are being unkind to one another, we can:

- Take a moment to remember how Jesus demonstrated the ultimate act of kindness in laying down His life for us while we were still sinners. Read Romans 5:8.

- To bring home Jesus' love for sinners, we can point our children to stories where Jesus showed kindness to even the most unkind people, like Zacchaeus. Read Luke 19.

- Then we can turn to Scripture that instructs our kids in living out Christlike kindness. Read Colossians 3:12.

When our children don't want to seek or grant forgiveness, we can:

- First, take a moment to remember that God has already forgiven every sin we have ever or will ever commit because of what Jesus did for us on the cross. Read Psalm 103:8-13.

Gratitude for God's grace is the greatest motivator for godliness.

- To bring home the forgiveness of Christ, we can point our children to stories where Jesus forgave others. For example, He forgave even Peter—who disowned and betrayed Him before His death. Read John 21:15-25.

- Then we can turn to Scripture that instructs our children in Christlike forgiveness. Read Ephesians 4:32.

When our children don't want to obey us or submit to our authority, we can:

- First, take a moment to remember how Jesus humbly submitted to His Father and obeyed Him, even unto death. Read Luke 22:39-44.

- Then we can turn to Scripture that instructs our children in obeying us and, ultimately, God. Read Ephesians 6:1.

2. RELY ON THE POWER HE GIVES THEM

As we teach our children to remember Jesus, we can also teach them to rely on Jesus. As I often remind my boys when they are struggling with a particular sin or weakness: *"But you belong to God, my dear children. You have already won a victory over those people, because the Spirit who lives in you is greater than the spirit who lives in the world"* **(1 JOHN 4:4, NLT).**

Read John 15:1-8. Who is the vine?

Who is the branch?

How does the branch produce fruit?

What produces more fruit?

How is God glorified?

In this passage, Jesus taught that we grow in holiness to the degree that we allow Jesus to take up residence in our hearts.

Apart from Him, we can do no good thing. He doesn't say we can do some good without Him. He says very plainly, *"Neither can you bear fruit unless you remain in me"* **(v. 4, NIV).** It's the indwelling of the Holy Spirit that produces the fruit of the Spirit in our children's lives.

> Read Galatians 5:22-23. What is the fruit of the Spirit?

We grow in holiness to the degree that we allow Jesus to take up residence in our hearts.

We can't produce the fruit of the Spirit on our own, and neither can our kids.

How often do I try to live in the likeness of Christ without relying on the power of Christ? Too often. But reminding my boys reminds me.

Apart from a living union with and utter dependence on God, we can do no good thing. We might be productive, but we won't be fruitful—and there is a profound difference in the two. God produces the fruit, for the glory and praise of His grace. Have no doubt: part of God's purpose for us is to produce fruit from us—fruit that will point others to the nature of God. And this fruit is produced in us only when we abide in and rely on Him.

3. RECOGNIZE HIS FAITHFULNESS TO GROW THEM

And then finally, as we teach them to remember Jesus and rely on Jesus, we can help our children recognize Jesus' work in their lives and His faithfulness to grow them.

I all too easily get stuck in a pattern of instructing and correcting, when I need to also be actively looking for, acknowledging, and affirming the fruit of God's grace in their lives. It's amazing how the countenance of my children changes when I recognize the fruit of the Spirit in their lives and point out that fruit specifically.

For example, I have a son who struggles with his temper. At night when we are all snuggled into our beds, he will often pray that God would help him control his temper and in his own words, "not get so angry." It's been a privilege to watch God slowly but surely answer that prayer in my son's life. I love being able to say, "I know that you just got really angry at your brother, and I want you to know how happy it made me to see you chose self-control in your response." Of course, there are and will continue to be circumstances in which he, like me, still loses his cool. He's human. But I love seizing any opportunity I can to show him how relying on the power of Christ within him empowered him to honor God in his response.

> Where do you see God working in the lives of your kids, and how can you encourage them to see God's faithfulness to grow them? Be as specific as possible.

Praise that recognizes the fruit of their salvation and points our kids back to Christ at work in their lives is always a good thing. It reminds them that it's Christ's work to save, sanctify, and strengthen us.

If we can keep *remember, rely,* and *recognize* in the forefront of our minds, then we will be set free from the pressure to control our children's behavior and transform their hearts. How freeing it is to know that as we seek to make the gospel central in our homes, it's the Holy Spirit's work alone to lead them in heartfelt trust and obedience.

Now, one last thing, OK? Because, we need to acknowledge this hard truth.

Our kids may very well take advantage of grace in the here and now. Is it safe to say we will too, at times? Ah yes, it's part of that whole being human thing.

And the likelihood of seeing the fruit of grace in our children's lives immediately is slim, right? The fruit of grace is almost always in the future. Parenting our kids with grace isn't a sprint; it's a marathon—a marathon worth running well.

Just because we give our kids grace does not mean it will penetrate their hearts on our time line and make them want to hang on to Jesus today because He hung on a cross for them 2,000 years ago. It might, but it might not.

What we do know for certain is that law-laden parenting is not what Scripture tells us will inspire or enable the human heart to devotion or obedience to God. It'll change behavior. But it won't change the heart. And ultimately, it can drive our kids away from their faith, because they will give up on ever being good enough to keep God happy.

Intentional, grace-based, gospel-centered parenting draws kids into the loving arms of their heavenly Father, who welcomes us at our worst and transforms rebellious hearts into radical followers of Christ.

CLOSE WITH PRAYER
Read Philippians 1:9-11, and write a prayer of response below.

God is using motherhood to draw us closer to His heart and to make our hearts more like His. A mom who experiences God's heart is a mom who is equipped to reflect God's heart to her kids. The love God pours into our hearts enables us to love and lead with His kind of love. So let us keep giving the gospel to ourselves, and making it central in our homes, as we rely on the power of the Holy Spirit to enlighten and transform our kids' hearts.

I want you to know I'm praying for you and your family. I'm praying with all my heart that the truth will continue to set you wildly free to live and parent in the fullness of His grace.

And finally, I'd love to pray with you, asking God to seal in our hearts all that He has shown us through these pages. Can we go to God together in prayer now?

CLOSE WITH PRAYER

Heavenly Father, You are beautiful. You are faithful and kind and compassionate and good. You are everything we need and everything our hearts long for. You are sovereign and full of grace. So we boldly come before You now and ask that You would help us ...

- believe we are Your beloved and help us overcome our disbelief;

- believe what You say over what we see;

- live by faith, not by sight;

- remember Your faithfulness in the past as we face the uncertainty of the future;

- desire the assurance of Your presence more than answers to our questions;

- lay down what You have not asked us to carry so that we can thrive in what You have;

- trust Your sovereignty over our significance in the lives of our children;

- make the good news of Jesus—not the good behavior of our children—the foundation on which we build;

- stop trying so hard and start enjoying the children You have entrusted to us more;

- rely on the Holy Spirit to produce the fruit of the Spirit in our kids' lives;

- be a reflection of Your heart and a vessel of Your love;

- parent with wonder over worry, faith over fear, connection over control, joy over anger, humility over pride, and love over shame; and

- finally, Lord, we ask You to impress upon our children a love for You that is anchored in Your great love for them.

Lord, more than anything else, help us nurture in them a sincere longing to know You, trust You, follow You, serve You, and love You—the only One who always has been and always will be their perfect Parent and sovereign Savior. We love You. We thank You. We praise and adore You. In Your beautiful and wonderful and powerful name we pray. Amen.

Breathe in grace, dear mom. You are covered. You are free.

Breathe in grace, dear mom.

#MOMSETFREE

FREEDOM TO LIVE YOUR CALLING

Group Discussion Questions

1. Review all the weeks of *Mom Set Free* and identify one truth you learned from each week.

2. What new freedom in Christ have you experienced that you can now extend to your children?

3. Why is heart change so important instead of just behavior modification?

4. Read Exodus 14:10-14. How do these verses apply to parenting?

5. What are some ways we can move forward in trusting obedience and do the work we need to do as moms?

6. What will you do to take the truths you've learned and incorporate them into your life and your parenting?

_____

_____

_____

_____

_____

_____

_____

_____

To hear more from Jeannie,
download the optional video
bundle at lifeway.com/momsetfree

LEADER TIPS

PRAY

Ask God to prepare you to lead this study. Pray individually and specifically for the women in your group. Make this a priority in your personal life and in preparation each week.

PREPARE

SECURE PASTOR AND STAFF SUPPORT. Talk with your pastor or the appropriate staff person if you want to teach this study as part of the ongoing ministry of your local church. Discuss together how it could best be used in the church. Ask for their input, prayers, and support.

SECURE YOUR LOCATION. Think about the number of women you can accommodate in the designated location. Reserve any tables, chairs, or media equipment for music or if you choose to use the optional videos.

PROVIDE CHILDCARE. This study is for moms. That means there are going to be children to be cared for. This is essential.

PROVIDE RESOURCES. Make sure you have the needed number of Bible study books. You might get a few extra for last-minute sign ups. Also, be sure to have the appropriate media equipment if you choose to use the optional video downloads.

PREVIEW EACH SESSION. Look over the content and the group discussion questions to prepare for the group discussion. Feel free to delete or reword the questions provided, and add other questions that fit the needs and circumstances of your group.

KNOW YOUR GROUP. You're probably going to have a group of moms who will be in different stages of life with different ages of children. Keep this in mind as you prepare, especially if you keep all the moms together in one large group. If you choose to use the optional videos, you might consider watching the video together and then splitting into separate groups according to the children's ages. If you choose that option, or another way to create small groups, you will need to secure leadership or mentor moms for each small group.

INFORM

Let moms know that some of the issues they face might be embarrassing or uncomfortable to discuss at times. Just agree together that it will take place and put it aside. Agree to confidentiality. The women need a safe place to discuss difficult issues of parenting.

STAY HUMBLE

Help moms understand that this is a time to be real with one another. Agree to have honest conversations with a willingness to discuss how we're struggling and even failing. Agree from the beginning that as a group we will discuss what we do right and the truth about mistakes and challenges.

EVALUATE

After each session and throughout the study, assess what needs to be changed to more effectively lead the study.

NEXT STEPS

Even after the study concludes, follow up and challenge moms to stay involved through another Bible study, church opportunity, or anything that will continue their spiritual growth and friendships.

TEACHING PLANS

SESSION 1: FREEDOM FROM THE PRESSURE TO BE ENOUGH

- Welcome moms to the study, provide name tags, and distribute Bible study books.

- Ask moms to share the names and ages of their children and why they were drawn to this Bible study.

- Give a short overview of the study, sharing the session titles and how there is personal study for them to do each week. Encourage moms to do what they can. If they are unable to complete all five days of the personal study, they can still learn and contribute in the group time each week. Help moms brainstorm specific times when they might try to complete their personal study each day.

- If you choose, watch the optional video.

- Discuss the questions on page 7 as a group.

- Close with prayer.

SESSION 2: FREEDOM FROM THE PLACES WE GET STUCK

- Welcome moms to Session 2 of *Mom Set Free*. Invite women to share one crazy mom story in pairs.

- Use the following questions to review their previous week's personal study.

  What are some of the lies you've believed as a mom?

  What are some of the battles you are facing that you desperately wish you could fix or control?

  Why is it so challenging to rest and trust in Jesus when you are a mom?

  How is your parenting changed when you spend time with Jesus?

- If you choose, watch the optional video.

- Discuss the questions on page 35 as a group.

- Close in a time of silent prayer. Ask women to pray specifically for their children.

SESSION 3: FREEDOM TO RECEIVE THE LOVE OF JESUS

- Welcome your group to Session 3 of *Mom Set Free*. Distribute strips of paper and ask women to write down one question they are grappling with as a mom. Invite volunteers to share their questions with the group and discuss how parenting does not come with a set of instructions. There is so much we learn along the way.

- Use the following questions to review Week 2's personal study.

  What is your role in parenting and planting seeds of faith in your children? What's is God's role?

  What are some examples of ways we can be open-handed in our parenting?

  What are powerful ways to teach responsibility and consequences to our children?

  How do you see yourself trusting in God's power and His promises?

- If you choose, watch the optional video.

- Discuss the questions on page 59 as a group.

- Direct women to pray in small groups. Encourage them to pray for one another and their children, trusting in God's power, promises, and plans.

SESSION 4: LIVING IN FREEDOM

- Welcome moms to Session 4 of *Mom Set Free*. Encourage women to share ways they've seen prayers answered since the beginning of the study.

- Use the following questions to review Week 3 of their personal study.

  What did you learn from Colossians 1:3-23 in your study this week?

  When and how have you struggled with this false equation that perfect equals lovable in your relationships with others and with God?

  In what area(s) of your parenting do you feel especially weak right now?

  What was most meaningful to you in your study this week?

- If you choose, watch the optional video.

- Discuss the questions on page 79 as a group.

- Pray for the moms and let them know you are available to talk and pray after the session if they have special prayer needs.

SESSION 5: FREEDOM IN TRANSFORMATION

- Welcome moms to Session 5 of *Mom Set Free* and begin by discussing a question from the homework this week: Why don't we like to think of ourselves as broken?

- Use these additional questions to review Week 4 of their personal study.

  In what ways does God's grace bring you the greatest comfort?

  What did the Scripture studied teach you about the way God looks at our brokenness?

  What character traits does grace produce in your life? How can you parent from under grace instead of parenting from under the law?

  What steps did you take this week to begin living as one loved by God?

- If you choose, watch the optional video.

- Discuss the questions on page 101 as a group.

- Close with prayer and encourage women to text, email, or call another mom this week and affirm the transformation you see in her.

SESSION 6: PARENTING IN FREEDOM

- Welcome your group to Session 6 of *Mom Set Free*. Acknowledge that sometimes talking about transformation is uncomfortable, but we hope we are all learning and growing as we continue to walk with Christ daily. Invite volunteers to share transformations they see in their kids or themselves.

- Use these additional questions to review Week 5 of their personal study.

  How did you acknowledge who you are apart from Christ this week?

  In what ways do you recognize Christ in your life? How are you becoming more like Him? How is that overflowing upon your children?

  How are you experiencing Jesus as your Good Shepherd?

  What are some ways you can experience victory over shame? How can you teach your kids the truth about shame?

- If you choose, watch the optional video.

- Discuss the questions on page 129 as a group.

- Close in prayer and encourage moms to complete their final week of homework before the last group session.

SESSION 7: FREEDOM TO LIVE YOUR CALLING

- Welcome moms to the final group time, Session 7 of *Mom Set Free*.

- Use these additional questions to review Week 6 of their personal study.

  Compare and contrast what parenting with grace looks like and what it does not look like.

  How can we reflect God's heart in the way we train and discipline our kids?

  How does thinking about the commandments and promises of Christ as gifts we give our kids change how we might approach discipline?

  What did you gain most from the four simple words—*what, why, how,* and *now*? How can they shift our focus in discipline?

- If you choose, watch the optional video.

- Discuss the questions on page 161 as a group.

- Encourage women to take some time to write a prayer on the next few pages for their children or specific prayers for each child. Play some soft music and allow women to pray and pour their hearts out to God. Close in prayer.

NOTES

NOTES

NOTES

ENDNOTES

SESSION 1

1. "Hope," *Evangelical Dictionary of Biblical Theology*, ed. Walter A. Elwell (Grand Rapids: Baker Books, 1996), 355.

SESSION 2

1. If you want to dig deeper into Romans 8:28 passage, Matt Chandler's sermon transcription "Village Identity—Part 8: God Saves," from October 9, 2011, is available at http://media.thevillagechurch.net/sermons/transcripts/201110091115FMWC21ASAAA_MattChandler_VillageIdentityPt8-GodSaves.pdf.

2. Oswald Chambers, *My Utmost for His Highest* (Grand Rapids, MI: Discovery House, 1992), June 26.

SESSION 3

1. Martin Luther and John Prince Fallowes, *Commentary on Galatians* (Grand Rapids: Kregel Classics, 1979), 6.

2. Beau Hughes, Sermon: "Galatians—Part 7: The Glorious Exchange," The Village Church (Denton, TX), March 25, 2012. Transcription available online at thevillagechurch.net.

3. Dennis E. Johnson, *Him We Proclaim: Preaching Christ from All the Scriptures* (Phillipsburg, NJ: P&R Publishing Company, 2007).

4. Tim Keller, *The Meaning of Marriage: Facing the Complexities of Commitment with the Wisdom of God* (Penguin Books, 2013).

5. Scott Sauls, "On Shame and Stewardship," *The Mother and Child Project: Raising Our Voices for Health and Hope* (Grand Rapids: Zondervan, 2015), 217-219.